THE *Grace* FACTOR

ALSO by ALAN COHEN

Are You as Happy as Your Dog?
A Course in Miracles Made Easy
Dare to Be Yourself
A Deep Breath of Life
A Daily Dose of Sanity
Don't Get Lucky, Get Smart
The Dragon Doesn't Live Here Anymore
Enough Already
Handle with Prayer
Happily Even After
Have You Hugged a Monster Today?
How Good Can It Get?
I Had It All the Time
Joy Is My Compass
Lifestyles of the Rich in Spirit
Linden's Last Life
Looking In for Number One
My Father's Voice
The Peace That You Seek
Relax into Wealth
Rising in Love
Setting the Seen
Why Your Life Sucks/What You Can Do about It
Wisdom of the Heart

The Grace Factor

Opening the Door

to Infinite Love

Alan Cohen

Alan Cohen Publications

P.O. Box 100

Kapaau, HI 96755 U.S.A.

www.alancohen.com

The Grace Factor: Opening the Door to Infinite Love/Alan Cohen.

ISBN 978-0-910367-03-5

Mensch: A Yiddish word meaning,
"a man of extraordinary character,
integrity, and heart."

This book is dedicated to
To Dr. Ned B. Stein,
a true mensch

Despair says I cannot lift that weight.

Happiness says I do not have to.

—James Richardson

My Grace is sufficient for you.

—2 Corinthians 12:9

Contents

Preface

A woman phoned my radio show and reported that years ago when she became pregnant, her doctors told her that the baby would not survive. She and her husband prayed fervently for the child's well-being, and the baby was born healthy and went on to live a happy life. Since that time she had a few miscarriages, and now the couple very much wants another child. "Do you think we each get a certain allotment of miracles, and when we use it up, we get no more?" she asked.

"That's not how it works," I told her firmly. "Miracles and well-being are our natural state, given freely without limit forever. Only the human mind lays bounds over the good available to us. It is not God's Grace we need to beg for. It is our own. And we don't need to beg. We just need to claim it."

From childhood, you and I were barraged with reasons for human sorrow. You've regularly heard about the sin factor, the guilt factor, the victim factor, the fate factor, the bad luck factor, the evil inclination factor, the human condition factor, the cruelty of nature factor, the accident factor, the pollution factor, the bully factor, the economic downturn factor, the bad government factor, the conspiracy factor, the being in the wrong place at the wrong time factor, and the just plain life sucks factor. If you listen to your parents, teachers, church, and the media, the cards are heavily stacked against any one of us, and humanity as a whole, escaping evil in one form or another. And if you enjoy yourself with too much chocolate, sex, or mai tais at beachfront hotels, you will pay in the afterlife. One way or the other, the devil will take his due.

Yet there is another factor we hardly ever hear about

that supersedes all the other factors and ills that seem to threaten us at every turn. It is the Grace factor. Grace is the more fundamental reality in which we are loved and cared for in ways that far surpass the dangers to which we feel vulnerable. It is a force more real and powerful than any evil the world can conjure, a light that shines away the shadows conjured by the fearful human psyche. Grace offsets sin, overcomes karma, lifts us beyond assault and attack, and takes us to a home more secure than any house we might inhabit. In the domain of Grace, love triumphs over sorrow and we emerge unsullied by the slings and arrows of outrageous fortune. We wake up from the dream of loss and separation and find that the scary stories we have been told are but grim fairy tales.

Grace is the greatest story never told because religions, theologians, and many spiritual teachers generally focus on the reasons we are so messed up and what we need to do to offset our iniquities. The *new* story, by contrast, is a love story with a far happier ending. This plot casts you not as a struggling peon eternally rolling a boulder up a hill, only to have it fall back on you. Instead, it honors you as godlike, innocent, and deserving of blessings. The new story recognizes your identity as the progeny of a Divine Parent who loves you not for what you do, but for what you *are*. The grander story spans far beyond sin and karma and sets your foot firmly on the unshakeable ground of Grace.

This book is a guide to discovering and receiving Grace even while you walk the earth. These truths are not associated with any one religion, although if you are religious, your faith will be affirmed here. Atheists, agnostics, skeptics, and cynics are equally welcome. Grace would be a poor host indeed to exclude anyone. By embracing all people and rising above accepted prescriptions for pain, we are entering a territory you have never been shown on a map of the world or the universe. Space is not the final frontier. Grace is.

In this book I will introduce you to the sorely underacknowledged Law of Grace and acquaint you with it so intimately that you rise beyond the vicious domain of human judgment. The Law of Grace transcends all the seeming laws human beings have fabricated to substitute for it. Perfectly scientific and impeccably practical, the Grace factor is available to anyone willing to claim it. The door is open and the welcome mat is laid before you. Are you ready to dwell in the vast territory revealed by the new story? If so, take my hand and let's step over the border together.

CHAPTER 1

The Sun Rose Anyway

ON A COLLEGE SPRING BREAK LARK, my girlfriend and I hopped a flight to Puerto Rico to drop in on the legendary *Mar y Sol* rock festival. We camped on a long white sand beach amidst thousands of revelers indulging in generous helpings of sex, drugs, and rock and roll. One night after my girlfriend fell asleep, I took a walk along the beach, where diehard partiers handed me an assortment of liquor and drugs, similar to the way spectators hand bottles of water to marathon runners. With extraordinary idiocy, I ingested whatever was put into my hand.

When the chemicals took effect, I tailspun into a paranoid hallucination. I believed that a group of local guys who had been hanging around the festival had raped and killed my girlfriend and they were coming after me. I plunged into the blackest pit of terror, certain I would not live to see the morning. My trip to the epicenter of hell seemed eternal.

Hours later, to my astonishment, I sat on a rock, looking at the ocean, and I watched the sun rise, the pink fingers of dawn caressing a tranquil sea. With those rays came incredible exhilaration and relief. The effects of the substances were wearing off and I was regaining clarity and sanity. I had lived through the night and none of my morbid fantasies had come to pass. I was all wrong about my nightmare.

Perhaps you, too, have found yourself trapped in a dark dream you fear you may not escape. Your search for your soulmate has left you lonely and frustrated; or your spouse has betrayed you; or your family has pressured you to follow the path they would prescribe for you rather than one you would choose; or you trudge daily to a job you hate; or you feel at the mercy of drinking, drugs, or smoking, and no matter how hard you have tried, you cannot shake the habit; or your bills are piling to the ceiling; or your body won't do what you want it to do; or wherever you turn there is bad news and suffering. On a global scale, lack, sorrow, and suffering have earmarked the long rocky journey of humanity, soured by war, disease, starvation, oppression, discontent, confusion, and struggle. Billions of people continue to plow through miserable lives, with no end in sight.

Yet what if, like me awakening from my paranoid delusion, there is a benevolent force that can and will lift you beyond your most difficult problems and guide you to higher ground? What if there is a way out from the dismal human condition we have come to accept as fixed and inescapable? What if all the bad dreams of your life are destined to give way to a morning sun as surely as my bad trip found me and my girlfriend alive and unharmed?

Grace is the recognition that fear is the liar. Behind the oppressive illusions that keep the world enslaved in despair, we are enfolded in well-being far beyond what our mortal minds can imagine. Grace is the undoing of the belief that the world is threatening at every turn and you must constantly protect yourself from predators. The flawed or horrid person you have been taught you are is but a sham identity laid upon you by people who projected their pain and fears onto you. The horror movie is but a play of images projected onto a screen; at some point the theater lights will go on and you will exit intact. Simply: the creations of darkness are void of truth, and impeccable wholeness is your abiding reality.

If it were up to me to work out my own salvation, I am inept. I have done many foolish things and made lots of errors I wish I could erase. I have acted unkindly and wielded heavy judgments against myself and others. I have turned my back on love and let the ego hijack important choices. I have travelled long gnarly detours from happiness and trusted teachers who proved false. I have questioned why anyone would choose to come to a domain as dark and dense as the world can be. If I were capable of mapping my healing, I would have escaped the human condition a long time ago.

Yet in spite of my doubts, flaws, and blunders, I have been sustained. Somehow my needs have been met and any trouble I have set in motion has been resolved. My life is a living lesson that Grace is the underlying condition of life and the benevolence of compassion far outshines our petty human judgments and the errors we have made. The hand of Grace holds us all. In spite of our blatant human frailty, the universe just keeps loving, healing, and supporting us. As it has been said, "God loves you and there's nothing you can do about it."

Sit with me, then, on a rock overlooking the ocean as dawn breaks. Remnants of nightmares may still ruminate in the hidden corridors of your psyche, but the majesty of the scene before you will shine them away. The dark time is gone and the light time is at hand. Together let us walk away from what seemed to be, and embrace what is.

Only the creations of light are real.
Everything else is your own nightmare.
—*A Course in Miracles*[1]

CHAPTER 2

From a Maze to Amazing

ON A BLEAK JANUARY NIGHT during the Great Depression, court was about to convene on the poor lower east side of Manhattan. Suddenly a gray-coated figure entered the courtroom and approached the bench. The visitor was Fiorello LaGuardia, flamboyant Mayor of New York City, who was known to ride on fire engines, read comics over the radio to the city's children, and drop in unexpectedly on sites of municipal services. LaGuardia informed the judge that he would be taking over the bench for the evening, and the judge went home.

The first case of the evening was that of an elderly woman accused of stealing a loaf of bread from a bakery. In her defense, the woman explained that she needed to feed her hungry grandchildren. The baker, outraged at the theft, demanded justice.

LaGuardia pounded his gavel and proclaimed, "I have no choice but to punish you. Ten dollars or ten days in jail." With that, the mayor threw ten dollars into his hat and passed the hat around the courtroom. "I hereby fine everyone present 50 cents each for living in a city where a grandmother has to steal a loaf of bread to feed her grandchildren." When the hat was returned, the woman paid her fine and took home an additional $47.50.

Even while the world is steeped in laws that bind human beings into ever smaller dungeons, Grace shines through the slightest crack offered it. Kindness melts the wall of loneliness, and separateness is suspended in the presence of love. No illusion is so thick that charity cannot dissolve it.

Kindness Trumps Threat

When Julio Diaz stepped off the No. 6 subway train in the Bronx, he was faced with a teenager pointing a knife at him. The mugger demanded Julio's wallet, which he gave willingly. As the robber began to flee into the night, Julio called to him, "Hey, wait a minute. You forgot something. If you're going to be robbing people for the rest of the night, you might as well take my coat to keep you warm."

Stunned, the boy turned and asked Diaz, "Why are you doing this?"

"If you're willing to risk your freedom for a few dollars, then I guess you must really need the money. I mean, all I wanted to do was get dinner. If you really want to join me . . . Hey, you're more than welcome."

In a real-life scene that would strain credibility as fiction, the two made their way to a diner where they sat in a booth, shared a meal, and talked about their lives. When Diaz asked the teen what he wanted out of life, he couldn't answer. He just displayed a sad face.

When the time came to pay the bill, Diaz told the fellow, "I guess that since you have my wallet, you're going to have to treat."

The young man gave Diaz back his wallet, Diaz paid for dinner, and gave the fellow $20. Diaz asked for something in return—the kid's knife—and he gave it to him. "If you treat people right, you can only hope they treat you right," Diaz later concluded. "It's as simple as it gets in this complicated world." (To watch a touching dramatization of this encounter, go to YouTube, *"Hey, You Forgot Something."*)

A Course in Miracles tells us that every thought, word, and action represents our choice between fear and love. When Julio Diaz encountered that mugger, the scenario could have led to many different outcomes, mostly dark. But when Diaz chose to view that potentially dangerous situation through the lens of kindness, he created an entirely different result than he would have generated if he had acted from fear. Healing, positive resolution, and miracles are the natural outcome of accepting and giving Grace.

Natural Miracles

The well-known song *Amazing Grace* was born of a miracle. The author of the song, John Newton, was a slave trader. One night in 1748 while at sea, his ship encountered a storm. The vessel began to fill with water and was well on its way to sinking. Newton prayed to God for help, and miraculously a load of cargo shifted its position and filled up the hole in the bow through which water had been entering. The ship sailed to safety, Newton a changed man. From that point on, he devoted his life to helping people, including slaves, rather than exploiting them.

When we recognize the presence of Grace, our life ceases to be a maze and becomes amazing. It morphs from terrible to terrific, from awful to awesome. When you change perspective, the results you generate are upgraded, sometimes quickly and dramatically. That LaGuardia courtroom became the setting for a higher justice, as did the subway platform where Julio Diaz met his mugger, and the hold of the ship where John Newton prayed. Likewise, your home, office, relationship, bank account, and body cease to be what they appeared to be a minute ago, and instead they become an arena for the magnification of kindness and the release from tyranny.

Grace is amazing to the fearful mind, but it is perfectly reasonable, even natural to the part of us connected to Higher Power. *A Course in Miracles* tells us, "Miracles are natural. When they do not occur something has gone wrong."[1] The misguided intellect has twisted reality into the opposite of truth. What is real seems unbelievable, and what is truly unbelievable—separation from God—is accepted as the status of life. Grace is the beacon that guides us home to our natural state. When we give Grace or receive it, we transcend the plight of humanity and fulfill our purpose as divine beings. This is the bread we need to take to our grandchildren.

There are only two ways to live your life.
One is as though nothing is a miracle.
The other is as though everything is a miracle.
—Albert Einstein

CHAPTER 3

Let Life Love You

AS COMMUTERS HUSTLED through the Washington, D.C. metro station on a cold winter morning, a musician stood next to a wall, playing his violin, the case at his feet open for donations. He played six Bach pieces over 45 minutes. A few people stopped and listened for a moment, then hurried on their way. Some threw some change or a dollar into the violin case. The most attentive listener was a three-year-old boy holding his mother's hand. He wanted to linger, but his mother tugged him along. Finally the musician retrieved $32 from the case, put his instrument away, and disappeared into the crowd. No one applauded or thanked him.

Not one of the passersby realized that the violinist was Joshua Bell, one of the world's most accomplished violin virtuosos. The pieces he played were extraordinarily demanding, performed on a Stradivarius violin worth almost four million dollars. Days earlier Bell had played to a sold-out crowd in Boston, tickets at $100.

Bell's impromptu concert was sponsored by *The Washington Post* as a social experiment to determine if listeners would recognize the talent before them if it was not identified. The commuters did not expect genius and they were busy hustling to work, so they overlooked the rare gift offered. Grace was given, but few received it. The little boy in the crowd was the only one attuned to the heavenly tones. Yet all could have stopped and received the gift, if they chose. "And a little child shall lead them . . ."[1]

Close Encounters of the Grace Kind

Is it possible that you have been showered with Grace your entire life, you are being showered with Grace now, and you will always be showered with Grace, but you have not realized it? *A Course in Miracles* tells us that the voice of healing is as loud as your willingness to listen.[2] The ecstatic Persian poet Kabir wrote, "I laugh when I hear that the fish in the sea is thirsty."

A caller phoned my radio show (hayhouseradio.com) and reported that years ago she went through a glorious phase in which everything she did worked like magic. She was in love, she felt alive and vital, her career flourished, and everything she touched turned to gold. She could do no wrong. Then something shifted and she slipped into a sense of struggle. She went through a marriage and divorce, her career sagged, and she developed health issues. Now, she explained, she was getting back into a positive flow, and she wanted some advice on how to stay in it. As we conversed, the woman voiced a realization far more profound than anything I told her. She said, "Maybe I have always been in the flow, and good has always been coming to me, but I just didn't realize it."

While God constantly gives Grace, we experience only as much as we let in. Someone gave me a pamphlet entitled, "*Are you Letting God Love You?*" That pamphlet sat on my coffee table for years, and every time I saw the title I had to answer that question for myself. It became an ongoing meditation. The question takes many forms: *Are you generous with yourself? Are you as kind to yourself as you are to others? Do you recognize you deserve the happiness your heart desires?*

Many people are happy to deliver Grace to others, but have a hard time receiving it. Yet when we see role models of others who show themselves kindness, we are more inclined to show kindness to ourselves. Here are some true stories of "Close Encounters of the Grace Kind" I have had with people who learned to love themselves as much as they had been loving others.

While I was presenting a seminar on prosperity, a woman posed this dilemma: "I am a Red Cross fundraiser. After a hurricane or flood, I swing into action and raise millions of dollars in a short time to aid the victims. Meanwhile, I'm struggling with my own finances and I have a hard time paying my bills each month. Why is that?"

I told her, "When you know that you deserve to have your bills paid as confidently as you know that the disaster victims deserve to have their needs met, you will raise the funds for your requirements as well as your joys."

My coaching client Todd served as a firefighter for 25 years. He decided to retire and he wanted to move from New Hampshire to Florida. "My wife and I are tired of the cold winters and we're ready for some sunshine," Todd told me. "We've arranged to rent a home in Florida for a month this winter." Then he added, "We'd really like to stay for three months."

"Then why don't you stay for three months?" I had to inquire.

"That seems like a lot to ask," Todd answered shyly.

I told Todd, "You have been saving people's lives for 25 years. You've courageously burst into burning buildings and rescued adults, children, their pets, and possessions. Many people are more grateful to you than to most other people in their lives. Don't you think someone who has helped so many people in such profound ways deserves to have three months in the sun—let alone the rest of your life?"

"When you put it like that, it makes sense," Todd replied.

A short time later Todd and his wife rented a house in Florida and they now spend half their time there each year.

A woman named Sara asked me if my Life Mastery Training in Hawaii would be helpful to her. "I worry about money, I yearn for a relationship, and I don't feel good," she told me.

I told Sara that she would be a prime candidate for the program. She agreed and attended. During the program, Sara experienced *aha!* moments that opened her to greater prosperity.

The day before the program concluded, Sara told me, "I just did something I have never done before. I phoned the airline and ordered an upgrade to first class for my flight home. It cost me $875—but I'm worth it!"

"Congratulations," I told her. "You just graduated from the training."

A few weeks later I phoned Sara to find out how she was doing. "Fabulous!" she told me. "I loved my first class flight, and when I got home I had a miracle. I was going through some financial papers and I found some unknown funds that equaled the cost of the training plus travel, including my upgrade."

To step into our true deservingness, we must question and challenge the beliefs in lack and unworthiness we have been taught, and find reasons for our greater deservingness. We are always arguing for our limits or for our possibilities, and we always get more of what we are claiming. The universe is just as willing to deliver riches of all kinds as it is to deliver lack and problems; actually the universe is *more* ready to deliver abundance than lack, for abundance is our natural state. When we open to receive our good, we are in alignment with the will of God, which is delighted to give us what we truly want and what it wants for us—which are the same.

Grow your Basket

If you would like to expand your capacity to receive, here is a powerful visualization I use in my seminars. Participants report that this helps them in a big way to allow more good into their lives.

Close your eyes and imagine you are sitting in a chair with a bowl or basket on your lap. This receptacle can be made of wood, wicker, ceramic, glass, crystal, or any other material you like.

In your vision, look up and see that there is no ceiling on the room in which you are seated. Instead, there is an infinite sky composed of a vast fountain of energy in the form of golden light. You are looking up at utter abundance.

This golden energy represents something you wish to have more of in your life: money; a rewarding relationship; a passion-filled career; robust health—anything you deeply value and yearn for. Now choose one element of life you would like to expand in your experience.

Imagine that the golden energy is pouring down to you like rain, all around you. As it flows down, you capture in your bowl or basket some of the energy or goal you desire. You are delighted to receive such substance of good. Meanwhile, notice there is much more substance pouring down around you than you are capturing in your container.

In your mind, now, expand your container. Push the edges of the bowl or basket outward by 25 percent. Now that your container is larger, you are receiving more of what your heart desires. Notice how good it feels to receive more.

When your container is full, expand it again so it grows even larger, to at least 50 percent more than its original size. You are capturing even more of your valued substance. Notice how rewarding it feels to let more good in!

When you are ready, expand your bowl one more time so it is twice its original size. Now your experience of prosperity is double what you started out with. What a wonderful feeling! Take some time to be with your expanded experience.

Now imagine that you can receive this light/energy/substance directly into your body.

Visualize it flowing in through the top of your head, then cascading like a waterfall down through your neck, shoulders, arms, hands, torso, hips, legs, and feet. *You* are the container for your good, and you are allowing yourself to be filled completely.

Take as long as you like to enjoy the feeling of receiving abundant prosperity.

When you are ready, return your awareness to your waking state, richly expanded in your capacity to receive what you value.

The Tide of Fortune

We succeed in life not just for what we *make* happen, but for what we *let* happen. If you believe that dark forces are working against you and you must battle your way past them like a swashbuckler swordfighting pirates on a gangplank, your life will be a constant struggle against evil. If, however, you believe there is a benevolent force seeking to love and support you, you will find *that* is so. Shakespeare proclaimed, *"There is a tide in the affairs of men, which, taken at the flood, leads on to fortune."*[3] That tide is *already* flowing on your behalf, but you must stand up on your surfboard and capture the wave rather than let it pass you by.

Grace often comes in unexpected ways, outside the box you have designed to capture your good. Do not limit your success to your plans, which are meager in comparison to life's greater plans for you. Be open to people and avenues through which your sustenance may arrive. Let abundance surprise you. The universe is simultaneously infinite in its capacity to support you, and ingenious in the ways it can find to do it.

Life is the great lover beckoning you to let it enfold you in its arms. Its gifts are available whenever you are ready. Might that be today?

CHAPTER 4

The Miracle of the Floating Fig

I ARRIVED AT HARBIN HOT SPRINGS at two o'clock in the morning. Quickly I peeled off my clothes and immersed myself in the soothing pool of body-temperature mineral waters. Soon I felt my tired muscles, stiff and aching after a long day's travel, unwind, caressed in liquid warmth. I found a seat on the underwater ledge, leaned my head back against the rim of the pool, and gazed into the starry night.

But I was famished. I had not eaten for many hours and, unable to find a store or restaurant during my late-night drive through the rural northern California mountain region, I arrived without any provisions. I began to feel anxious about not being able to get anything to eat until the next day. Then I looked around me and realized I was in a place of great tranquility. A burning candle radiated its mellow glow on a nearby ledge while a mountain stream chanted a lullaby a few yards from the pool. Surely God was in this place. Though there were no people present, I was not alone. I may not have had physical food, but spiritual nourishment abounded.

Just then my reveries were interrupted by something touching my lip—an object had floated toward me and bumped into my mouth. I reached to remove it, and discovered it was a fresh fig! You can imagine my delight to find a sweet delicacy—actually, it found *me*—in the middle of a hungry night. In rhythm with the grace of the moment, I opened my mouth and received communion from a provident universe.

Then I looked up to see I was sitting beneath a huge fig tree that spread its leafy limbs out over my entire section of the pool! Below the tree I found many figs, freshly fallen, floating on the surface of the pool. I gathered a handful and went on to savor a most treasured midnight snack.

There is no place devoid of the love and presence of God. Providence goes with you and finds you wherever you are. Because God is within you, you take God wherever you go. Thus it is impossible for you to be alone or outside the domain of Grace. *A Course in Miracles* asks us to remember, "I am content to be wherever He wishes, knowing He goes there with me."[1]

What You Need When You Need it

The spiritual teacher Bashar[2] defines abundance as:

The ability to do what you need to do when you need to do it.

True prosperity does not stipulate a particular amount of money in your bank account, a specific job, a certain marriage partner, or any other condition as a prerequisite for being or feeling abundant. It simply means that the universe is always capable of supplying your needs, and it will, if you let it. The best manifestations of abundance show up in the moment, unplanned, undictated, and unorchestrated by the reasoning mind. Providence loves to surprise you.

If you knew that you are being taken care of and you always will be, would you need to plot the means by which your good will arrive? Would you need elaborate defenses to protect you from ill-intending forces? Would you need a plan for your life based more on fear than faith? Faith does not force, horde, or gather armies or arsenals. It allows the love of God to be our singular Source at every new moment, able to reach us through an infinite number of channels.

But you must be reachable. The more you anxiously scheme to create or protect your well-being, the less able the universe is to find and serve you, try though it might and able though it is. Childlike faith is a more powerful asset than all the portfolios and weapons the world might provide. Stuff does not ensure happiness; often it distracts us from the riches we already own. Only Spirit ensures happiness. When you want peace more than protection, you shall have both.

The Bottomless Pot

I was once in a relationship with a woman who wanted to take an expensive healing training. At the time, I was earning the income for us as a couple. The training she wanted to take required a high tuition, plus numerous trips to a far distant location, at significant travel expenses. My initial reaction was to resist laying out such a large sum of money. I told her so, and we argued.

That night I had a dream in which I was at a party where I was serving spaghetti from a large pot to a group of people. The recipients were lined up with their plates, filing past me, eager to be fed. Some were coming back for seconds. I began to be concerned that I would run out of spaghetti to feed them. But then a miracle occurred. No matter how many plates came before me, and how low the volume of spaghetti in the pot appeared to be, whenever I dipped my serving spoon into the pot, there was enough spaghetti to feed the person standing before me. After a while I realized that there would always be enough spaghetti, so I took joy, not fear, in feeding everyone.

When I awoke it was clear to me that the dream was a profound teaching in abundance of resources. I did not have to worry about the cost of my partner's training draining our reserves. We would be taken care of by the hand of Providence. So I told her that I would be happy to support her to take the training, which she deeply appreciated. This was one of the greatest lessons in abundance that I have ever received, which has yielded extremely practical results. Even though the experience occurred many years ago, I often remember it and apply it if I feel fear around money or enoughness. The Source has never failed me, as it will not fail anyone who taps into the bottomless pot.

Beyond Explanation

A woman from Australia wrote me this letter:

> I had heard about your book *The Dragon Doesn't Live Here Anymore*, and I tried to find it, but at the time it had not yet been released in Australia. So I just resigned myself that I would have to wait until it came out.
>
> One morning I took the bus into Sydney on my way to work, and upon exiting the bus I had to cross a huge intersection to get to my office. As I was making my way across

> the street, hordes of people bustling in both directions, my foot kicked something. I looked down to find, to my amazement, a copy of *The Dragon Doesn't Live Here Anymore.* The chances of this happening are absolutely infinitesimal. I now know without a doubt that Spirit provides for all of my needs in astounding ways.

Don't try to figure out how the universe can or will take care of you. Simply let your good to be doled out to you according to Divine Plan. The ego's plan will not get you there. Spirit's plan will. Your sustenance can arrive through any of an infinite number of channels.

I once went to visit a friend and found him listening to an extraordinary motivational lecture on a cassette tape. The talk was one of the most brilliant and exhilarating I had ever heard. When the lecture was over I asked him, "Who was that speaking?"

"I have no idea," he answered.

"Where did you the get tape?"

"At Radio Shack."

"Radio Shack is selling motivational tapes?"

"No, they aren't. I bought some blank cassette tapes there. When I opened the new package, this was one of them."

Grace often defies the known laws of science, but more accurately it complies with higher laws. Grace works through the avenue of synchronicity, not probability. *A Course in Miracles* reminds us, "I am under no laws but God's."[3]

Through the Lens of the Miraculous

Winston Churchill said, "A pessimist sees the difficulty in every opportunity; an optimist sees the opportunity in every difficulty." The universe becomes magical when you observe it through the lens of the miraculous. My sense of awe is expanding daily; I am recapturing the wonder of childhood, which faded from my life when I was taught that if I wanted something good to happen, I had to struggle to get it. Now I know that something good is always happening, and the more I recognize it, the more I potentiate benevolent manifestation.

Theologian Abraham Joshua Heschel wrote a book entitled, *God in Search of Man*. We do not have to search for God; we just need to let God find us. My fig miracle was not an exception to the laws of life; it was the *fulfillment* of them.

We do not need to acquire worthiness. We just need to release the false beliefs that stand between us and the good we deserve. The time will come when we will put aside "the toys of childhood," as the apostle Paul described[4] and take up the mantle of spiritual maturity. When we allow the small self to be supplanted by the Great Self, all the love, wisdom, and power we sought through worldly ambition flows to us without anxious manipulation.

In the classic film *The Wizard of Oz*, the Wicked Witch of the West skywrites an ominous message: *Surrender Dorothy*. While the witch scribed the warning from her gnarly ego, it contains a more profound injunction: Surrender, Dorothy, to the Power that can guide you through this ordeal. Surrender to the wisdom, courage, and heart you already own. No green-faced witch, wacky monkey army, or fake wizard can give you or take from you the well-being the universe has invested in you.

If you are struggling with a financial, career, relationship, or health issue, at this moment the universe is writing a message to you in the sky, in huge unmistakable letters: *Surrender,* ____________________ [Fill in your name]. Surrender to the love that wants to care for you in ways you cannot care for yourself. Surrender to people and forces that truly want to help you. Surrender to the worthiness you already own. Then, precisely at the moment you give up complaining about being hungry and you recognize the vast sustenance in and around you, a fig from nowhere will touch your lips and you will be fed.

> But, all this while, I was giving myself very unnecessary alarm. Providence had mediated better things for me than I could possibly imagine for myself.
>
> —Nathaniel Hawthorne

CHAPTER 5

The Face of God

DOES GOD KNOW YOU? Does anyone hear your prayers and answer them? Is there Someone out there who cares about you and wants to help you heal and improve your life? Or is the universe just a matrix of scientific principles, wisely set in motion perhaps, yet ultimately impersonal?

One day I received a mysterious DVD in the mail from Netflix. The title, *The Secret Things of God*, was not one I remembered ordering. Curious, I popped the disk in my player and discovered it was a seminar presented by a Christian psychologist. I am generally leery of Christian movies, since many of them dip into dogma, fire, brimstone, and Christian superiority for deserving salvation. But this one seemed innocuous enough, so I gave it a chance.

At one point the speaker addressed the Law of Attraction. He stated [my paraphrase here] that the Law of Attraction as taught, understood, and practiced by most people, does not generally take into account the personal nature of God and our relationship with Him. While God expresses through scientific principles, God also embodies attributes of love, kindness, caring, nurturing, and mercy, and has a very real relationship with us, His beloved children. The universe is much more than scientific. The universe is the greatest love story of all time.

This perspective touched me deeply. It was a holy vitamin often missing from teachings that portray God as principle only. Yes, God is science. And yes, God is love. Science is incomplete without the acknowledgment of the very real relationship between Creator and Its creation.

Grace is the hallmark of the divine love that sustains us without condition or judgment. In this chapter we will explore the ways that God reaches into the world with a kind hand, and cares for each of us personally and individually.

Angels Among Us

Angels don't always bear wings or arrive on puffy clouds accompanied by a trumpeted hallelujah chorus. More often they walk among us in familiar forms, used by Higher Power as channels for blessing and healing.

One day while driving into town I picked up a woman hitchhiking with a small dog. To my dismay I found that the woman was quite drunk. She rambled on senselessly, her little Chihuahua "Peanut" sitting stoically on her lap.

Finally we arrived at her destination and she got out of the car. As she stumbled toward a lamppost, I winced and worried that she would bring harm upon herself. Then I watched Peanut "round her up." He stayed at her feet, guiding and protecting her. An inner voice spoke to me: "Peanut is her guardian angel. He signed up to take care of her."

Sometimes guardian angels show up as people, or pets, or they come in dreams or whisper in your ear. It is rare that divine messengers stream from the heavens as depicted in the Bible or movies. Yet their earthly presence and deeds are no less glorious. People and animals serve as emissaries of God in the world. The face of God is the face of anyone we truly love, or who loves us, or who helps us in a time of need.

Many people want to know the names of their guardian angels or spirit guides. Such seekers are looking in the wrong place. The name of your guardian angel is the name of your child, or the agent at the post office who gives you your mail when you have forgotten your post office box key, or the school that gives you a scholarship when you can't afford the tuition. It is the name of the driver who pulls off the road to offer you help when your car has broken down, or the policeman who lets you go rather than writing you a ticket. If you examine your life carefully, you will realize that you have had many, many guardian angels, and you have seen the face of God many times.

The Servant and the Holy Man

A spiritual seeker heard about a holy man who lived high in the Himalayas. This guru, it was said, could change a person's life if he or she spent even two minutes in the sage's presence. The seeker, hungry for enlightenment, decided to make the long and arduous journey. He traveled halfway around the world, scaled enormous mountains, forged through howling winds and blinding snow, went without food for days, narrowly escaped wild beasts, and finally arrived at the holy man's house atop a remote peak.

As he approached, he found a long line of people waiting to get in. The seeker took his place and waited for his opportunity to advance. Finally he reached the door of the house, where he was greeted by a servant.

"I have come to meet the holy man!" said the traveler.

"Yes, please come in."

Once inside, the seeker scanned the house for sight of the sage. But he was nowhere to be found. Meanwhile the servant tried to make conversation with him. He asked the seeker what had motivated him to come so far at such an effort to meet the saint, and how he would like the master to help him.

Anxiously anticipating his time with the saint, the seeker gave the servant brief, perfunctory answers. The servant patiently guided the man through several rooms, and finally led him to a door and opened it. To the visitor's surprise, the door led outside.

"Thank you for coming," the servant told the man.

"But wait!" the seeker complained. "I have come all this way to see the holy man. Can I see him for just two minutes?"

"You just did," the "servant" stated quietly, and closed the door behind the man.

Enlightened people rarely hold a neon sign up over their head, proclaiming, "I am a great spiritual guru." Authentic saints are seamlessly woven into the fabric of life, disguised as waitresses, van drivers, appliance repairmen, bank clerks, and yard helpers. To see the face of God, do not be distracted by titles, degrees, glitzy demonstrations of power, or accoutrements. The face of God is not guaranteed by a flowing robe, but by the light of the soul. Stay attuned to the spirit, and you will meet God on a daily basis, in the most normal of places.

Windows to Heaven

Our culture is technologically overfed but spiritually malnourished. Scientific knowledge has advanced faster than the wisdom to use it. We have rocketed to the moon but not risen above nationalism, religious superiority, and prejudice. We have plumbed the depths of the ocean, but hide in the shallows of our hearts. We have photographed every inch of the earth, but the picture of why we are here remains undeveloped. We've figured out how to move masses of people at astonishing speeds, but we have not figured out why so many people are depressed and dispirited and don't want to go to the jobs to which mass transit delivers them. Japan's bullet trains, for example, are among the fastest and smoothest modes of transport on the planet. Japan also has one of the highest suicide rates in the world. What's the use of taking people places faster if they just kill themselves when they get there?

In a world that is rapidly becoming more technical and less personal, we must find more value in each other than in our toys. If you spend your dates texting or you are married to your smartphone, it is going to be difficult to develop a relationship with a partner. Technology is a dual-edged sword. It has a phenomenal capacity to bring us together, but an equally phenomenal capacity to distract and separate us. Intention makes the difference. I sometimes fantasize about what would happen if the entire Internet and all wireless technology were disabled for a day. OMG, we would then have to relate to each other! We might have to actually talk to each other over meals, look each other in the eyes, and communicate with our lips rather than our thumbs. Then what would we do?

The connection we seek is available to us whether or not our smartphones are working. Our family, friends, co-workers, and the hotel desk agent all offer windows to heaven if we choose to look through them. God is in the Internet, but It is even more profoundly present on the In-nernet.

Even while we stream countless bytes of data around the planet, we suffer from connectile dysfunction. The answer to our personal and planetary woes is not more gadgets. The answer is more connection. There is a form of wireless communication that supersedes what our smartphones use. It transmits and receives at the frequency of the heart. When we attune to that channel, we will arrive at where we hope all of our devices will take us.

Shifting the Lens

In some of my seminars I conduct an exercise that enables participants to see the face of God. You can perform this simple process if you wish. If you like, put on some soft background music to enhance the experience.

> Choose a partner and sit facing him or her at the closest distance at which you are both comfortable. Without speaking, look at your partner's face. Notice his or her physical appearance. Be aware of your partner's gender, age, and bodily presentation. What is your partner's ethnicity or race? His or her hair color and style? Prominent facial features? What physical characteristics draw your attention?
>
> Meanwhile your partner is noticing your physical appearance. He or she is looking at your face, hair, skin, body size, and shape. You are using the physical domain to make a statement about your identity. Take a minute now to establish yourself in the vision of the physical. If you feel any anxiety, take a long, slow, deep breath.
>
> (Pause)
>
> Now, as if shifting the lens of a microscope to a deeper magnification, consider your partner's

personality. Is this person talkative or quiet? Gregarious or shy? Serious or funny? Bold or timid? Intellectual or emotional? A leader or a follower? How would you describe your partner's personality to someone who did not know him or her?

Notice any other criteria by which you might label your partner's personality, such as his or her astrological sign, hyperactivity, obsessiveness, or any other social-psychological diagnosis or label that might apply to them. How does this person cope with upset or pain? What is their predominant style of presentation to the world?

Remember that your partner is simultaneously assessing your personality traits and labels. Simply notice without judging. Again, if you feel nervous, breathe deeply.

(Pause)

Now shift the microscope lens again and consider how your partner thinks and what he or she believes. We are now stepping in the mental realm. Is your partner's thought process clear or scattered? What intellectual pursuits might he or she excel at? What books does this person read? What is their religion? What is their political affiliation? What does this person believe about how life works and his or her place in it?

Your partner is simultaneously observing your intellectual style and choices; what you believe and how you see the world. Just let these traits be, for better or worse, and notice them as a dispassionate observer.

Now shift the lens of the microscope one more time and go beyond any and all physical, personality, or mental labels. Let your vision reveal your partner's inner spirit. If you look into this person's eyes clearly and deeply, you will see radiant energy. Your partner is so much more than body, emotions, and mind. He or she is a living spirit, an expression of God in life.

Take a few moments now to establish yourself in your spiritual vision of your partner. See this person as energy more than form; life more than the vessel through which life expresses. See your partner as a pure expression of God, perfect just as he or she is.

At this moment your partner is seeing the beauty, magnificence, and perfection of your spirit as well. He or she is seeing the God in you, as you. Both of you are God seeing God through the eyes of God.

Take a few more moments in silence to dwell in the presence of the divine as it is expressing through you and your partner. You are both so much more than your bodies, personalities, emotions, and minds. You are love discovering itself.

(Pause)

When you are ready, gradually return to your awareness of your identity as two partners in this room, and take a few minutes to describe your experience with each other.

Many participants report that this exercise is one of the most profound experiences of the seminar, and even of their life. We have become so identified and immersed in our physical, emotional, mental, and social identities that we have lost contact with our true identity as expressions of the divine. The awareness of inner spirit you gain through this exercise, or however you choose to find it, is the only one that matters and that will bring you peace.

The Ultimate Encounter

When I visited a Shinto shrine in Japan, I was fascinated to observe the design of the temple. In contrast to many ornate churches, this sanctuary was simple, open, and natural. When I approached the altar, I expected to find some statue, artifact, or religious symbol. Instead, at the center of the altar, at face height, was a mirror. I was astounded! I have never before seen a mirror in the holiest spot on a religion's altar.

The message was unmistakable: If you want to see the face of God, look in a mirror. While we find joy in seeing the face of God in others, our ultimate fulfillment is to see the face of God as our own. Can you believe that God dwells within you, shines through your eyes, and speaks through your lips? If not, you don't know God and you don't know yourself. To know your Self is to know God.

Most people fear to look upon the face of God because they have learned to associate God with fear and punishment. Yet to see God would not mean your death. It would mean only life. You do not have to wait until you depart this world to look upon God's face. It is available in the face of everyone you see, including your own. We need not look into outer space or to invisible angelic realms for redemption. It is here. It is us.

> In the faces of men and women I see God,
> and in my own face in the glass;
> I find letters from God dropped in the street, and
> every one is signed by God's name . . .
>
> —Walt Whitman[1]

CHAPTER 6

The End of Sin

HOW MANY SINS DO YOU HAVE? Have you done so many bad things that you fear or expect you will go to hell? Is there any way you will ever pay off all of your sins?

Yours sins will not end when you have suffered to pay for them, or when you become so saintly that you don't have any. Your sins will end when you realize that you never had any. Change your mind about what you believe are your sins, and they will haunt you no more. When you realize that your supposed sins were just errors, and the growth you gained through those experiences has contributed to your awakening, iniquities are transformed to blessings.

Sin is a singled-out thought of the past; a darkly chosen perspective; the cruelest of self-interpretations. When you focus on what you believe to be your sins, you are seeing an extraordinarily narrow interpretation of yourself. You dredge up the harshest possible past and claim it as your identity. You are filtering the glorious light that you are through the lens of judgment, and claiming evil as the truth about you. *It is not so*. At any moment you can shift your identity to that of an innocent divine being, without sin entirely. Karma is not a burden you labor to offset. It is a belief you rise beyond. God does not see your sins. God knows only your beauty, infinite worth, and holiness. All claim of sin is an attempt to defy and deny the will of God, which is your inherent purity. You will not succeed at this impotent rebellion. As the title of a famous play affirms, "Your arms are too short to box with God." Ultimately only your wholeness prevails. Your arguments against yourself will be thrown out in the Higher Court. *A Course in Miracles* tells us that the only verdict God will pass down upon you is "case dismissed."[1]

Sex in Public, Dinner behind Closed Doors

The belief in sin is socially programmed. What constitutes a sin in one culture may be entirely acceptable, even laudable in another culture. In the early 1900's anthropologist Bronislaw Malinowski travelled to the Trobriand Islands in the South Pacific to study that culture's mores. What he found was astonishing: The Trobriand Islanders had very free sex lives before marriage, including group sex. Sexual activity was encouraged in children, girls from the age of four to six and boys from the age of ten to twelve. From our cultural viewpoint, this may seem unbelievable, outrageous, and even sinful. But the Trobriands held it all very lightly. Yet despite their sexual libertarianism, there was one strict taboo no Trobriand would ever consider violating: Sharing a meal with one's intended mate before marriage. That's right: Premarital sex—have all you want. Premarital meal—*fuggetaboutit*!

Living in Hawaii, I have learned about the culture and spiritual practices of the ancient native Hawaiians, who had a very lighthearted and playful attitude toward sex. Many hula dances express stories that are multi-tiered in meaning. Certain hand, hip, and feet movements refer to a particularly fragrant flower, while also referring to venerating the king's genitals. These people lived in harmony with nature, had no hang-ups about sex, and their culture was extremely happy.

Enter the missionaries, who dressed up the natives in dense Victorian attire, told them sex was evil, and led them to believe they would go to hell unless they accepted Jesus Christ as their savior. Enter sailors who introduced venereal disease, measles, and whooping cough into a pure non-immune culture, killing a huge percentage of the native Hawaiians. The hula was outlawed, along with the Hawaiian language and other cultural traditions. Nothing like a good dose of civilization to destroy a culture living in harmony with each other and nature.

Fast forward to the 21st century, in which religions that define sexual impulses as sinful still thrive. Fact: The states in which fundamentalist religion is the most prevalent are also the states that register the highest use of Internet pornography. If you judge natural impulses as evil, and frighten or legislate people out of expressing them, you do not extinguish the behavior. You simply drive it underground, to be played out in surreptitious ways.

Anything you label as a sin will bounce back with vengeance. "The only problem with troubleshooting is that trouble shoots back." Those who fight the devil don't realize that the surest way to keep an undesirable habit in force is to feel guilty about it. Guilt does not extinguish unwanted behavior. It reinforces it. Guilt may force the recipient to hide or attempt to squash the judged behavior, but unless you come to terms with the *source* of the behavior, it will just pop up elsewhere.

To end aberrant or socially destructive behaviors, we must downplay punishment and amplify reward; drop guilt and celebrate our innate divine creation; disidentify with the dismal labels cast upon us, and claim our inherent purity. We must teach our children their enoughness rather than their deficiency. We must validate them for who they are rather than criticize them for who they are not. We must fan the flame of their uniqueness rather than teaching that they gain value only by comparison and competition. Children who feel nourished at a soul level do not grow up into adults who barge into elementary schools and shoot innocent children. Someone who would perform such a heinous act is deeply wounded at the soul. You can't scare or punish people into compassion, happiness, or morality. But you can love them so deeply that they do not lash out in frustration in futile attempts to offset the pain that kindness would have healed.

Sin or Error?

The word "sin" is a translation from the original Hebrew that predates English versions of the Bible by thousands of years. In that language the word for sin is *"avera"*—an archery term that means "to miss the mark." It says nothing about eternal damnation. It simply indicates, "You didn't hit the bulls-eye this time. Try again."

A "sin" implies that you have done something so egregious that it can never be corrected and you are doomed to punishment because of it. An "error" implies that you made a mistake which you can and will correct. Sins mean you will never get another chance. Errors means you get do-overs until you master the task at hand.

When I was growing up, my Catholic friends were not allowed to eat meat on Friday—that was a sin. Then one day a group of men had a meeting and announced that eating meat on Friday was no longer a sin. Hearing that, I scratched my head and wondered, "Who is making up these rules?" Such "laws" issued from human opinion, not God. It seemed to me that the Catholic Church was being run more like a condo association than a religion. The principles that govern life are more fundamental and stable than any that can be altered by a vote of men.

Universal laws are based on love, and have nothing to do with sin and punishment. They boil down to a few basic themes: You are an eternal, indestructible being created in the image and likeness of a whole, perfect, and loving God. Fear not. The God who created the heavens and the earth has your back.

Unnatural Selection

The Bible, while certainly containing the word of God, has also been injected with the fear and guilt that taints the minds of human beings. While many fundamentalists love to quote frightening fire and brimstone threats, there are just as many statements of our innocence and worthiness. To truly make the Bible work on our behalf, we must select the passages that lead us to peace, not hell.

In the famous parable[2], Jesus came upon a mob of angry men about to stone a woman caught in the act of adultery. He told them, "Let the one among you who is without sin cast the first stone." The crowd dissipated and he asked the woman, "Where are they now? Has no one condemned you?"

"No one, my Lord," she answered.

"Then neither do I condemn you," said Jesus.

This parable is one of Jesus's greatest hits. I wish it were quoted as often as the scary verses and stories. To truly understand the Bible, we must recognize the incident as a metaphysical teaching more than an historical account. It goes far beyond religion, into depth psychology. Our condemners are not so much people as they are the thoughts with which we condemn ourselves. If other people condemn you, they are reflecting your own self-judgments.

If you did not condemn yourself, you would not encounter the judgments of others, or if they did show up they would not affect you. If someone's criticism bugs you, part of your mind agrees with them. It is not *their* judgment that hurts; it is *your* agreement. When Jesus asked the woman, "Where are they now?" he was referring to her thoughts of self-condemnation. He was calling her—and us—to rise into the vision of innocence he held; to step into the Christed part of her own mind, and ours, that says, "neither do I condemn you." When we can see ourselves and the world through his eyes of reprieve, not condemnation, we achieve the great homecoming.

Life Beyond Sin

You cannot do anything so heinous that you would insult God or tear the fabric of the universe. You can think thoughts and perform acts that fortify your sense of separation, abandonment, and loneliness. You can forget who you are and dream you are adrift in an angry sea. But dreams have meaning and power only while you sleep. When you awaken, the churning swells disappear and you find yourself in the comfort and safety of your bed. Even while you *seem* to wander in a far country, you carry your home with you.

The end of sin will not come when you *become* good. The end of sin will come when you realize that you *are* good. Becoming good is not an act that occurs in time. It is an elevation of awareness that transpires in the sacred now. While you must consider any pain your acts cause others, it is even more significant to consider the pain that caused you to do those acts. Your own healing is the prerequisite to transform all of your relationships. Your peace is the gift you bring to the world, worth cultivating above all else.

We are graduating from the dark time. You know too much to turn back now. Throw off the cloak of sin and stand in the dignity of your true identity. God weeps to consider the pain you have accepted as necessary, and the threats you have deemed formidable. Religions or the elements of religion that dote on sin will not survive. Humanity is emerging into a new maturity based on validation, not torture. Teach yourself that you have not sinned, and you will free yourself. Teach others that they have not sinned, and you will free the world.

All your past except its beauty is gone,
and nothing is left but a blessing.
—*A Course in Miracles*[3]

CHAPTER 7

The End of Punishment

AT THE AGE OF FOURTEEN I adopted Orthodox Judaism as my spiritual path. I dove headlong into the many rules, rituals, and practices of this ancient complex religion. I went to the temple regularly, observed the Sabbath, ate kosher food, prayed three times a day, and during prayer I wore *tephilin*, a set of small boxes containing a parchment from the Torah. I found deep meaning and a warm sense of community in my religious pursuit.

Yet part of me feared that God would punish me if I didn't toe the line. On some days I did not say all the prayers and I did not don the tephilin. Feeling guilty, I cornered the synagogue president, Charlie Bolton, a younger and more progressive fellow than many of the temple elders. "Mr. Bolton, what happens if you do not put on the tephilin?" I asked him, readying myself for his recitation of a stiff penalty. Mr. Bolton thought for a moment, smiled, and answered, "They lay in the bag."

Oh.

Little did I realize that this kind man was planting within me a seed of Grace that would sprout and grow as I matured. The God Charlie Bolton knew was not a wrathful, punitive tyrant who smites sinners for not doing the practices meticulously. The God *he* knew was a generous, forgiving Creator who loves us for who we are, not what we do.

God is not Angry at You

The Finger of God is a documentary film about people who perform miracles, including faith healers. The movie introduces a young man who has taken it upon himself to be an evangelist on college campuses. He approaches students, especially those who appear injured, and offers to pray for them and heal them. In some cases he achieves remarkable results. In the film he made a statement to one student that got my attention:

"God is not angry at you."

As I heard those words, I realized how much of my life I have feared that God is or would be angry at me. I was afraid to do lots of things because they might incur God's punishment. To consider "God is not angry at you" opened for me a portal of release of cosmic proportion.

If you believe that God is angry at you and it's just a matter of time until "the other shoe drops," *think again.* No punishment awaits you. Only love awaits. In the movie *The Mission*, Mendoza is a slave trader in South America who kidnaps natives from an indigenous tribe in the mountains and sells them to plantation owners. When Mendoza finds his brother in bed with his own fiancée, he flies into a fit of rage and kills him. Overcome with remorse, Mendoza enters a monastery and takes on the self-imposed penance of carrying an enormous sack of heavy metal weaponry everywhere he goes. One day he scales the towering Iguaçu Falls with his cumbersome sack tied to his waist. When he reaches the plateau at the top of the waterfall, he encounters the tribe from which he had kidnapped slaves. A tribesman approaches him and raises a huge sharp knife. Seeing this, Mendoza bares his breast, awaiting execution. But the tribesman does not plunge the knife into Mendoza's heart. Instead, he cuts the rope that attaches Mendoza's heavy sack to his body, and hurls it over the cliff. In a poignant symbolic scene, we see the burden of penance plummet down, down, down into the abyss and disappear into the river far below. Liberated from his self-inflicted penalty, Mendoza learns the meaning of forgiveness. He then devotes the rest of his life to championing the cause of the natives he once exploited.

We, too, carry a heavy burden of penance and expected punishment. But it is not God who plunges the knife into our breast. It is we who do that to ourselves. God is the one who casts the sack over the cliff.

A Course in Miracles tells us, "*All that you believe will come of your sins will never happen.*"[1] This is a promise worth contemplating whenever you fear punishment by God. Ask yourself, "Am I Mendoza awaiting execution, or am I the forgiving tribesman who offers Grace?"

Shame Off You

Guilt is not a natural emotion. It is entirely learned; programmed; taught; instilled. No child is born with guilt. Children enter the world in a state of boundless purity. They have not yet been taught what is wrong with them, what they need to do to prove themselves, and how they must strive to earn love. We are attracted to be with children because they retain the awareness of their original innocence. They are still connected to heaven. If you are a parent or you have been around children, you understand this. By contrast, guilt is adopted like a shabby, tattered, foul-smelling, heavy coat laid over innocent shoulders until they become weighted and downtrodden.

My friend's young son came home from Sunday school and told her that he needed to take a bath. "Why do you need to take a bath?" she asked him.

"I think I got something on me in Sunday school that I have to get rid of," he explained.

"And what is that?"

"I said something the teacher didn't like, and she told me, 'Shame on you.' Whatever that is, it doesn't sound good."

Shame has been projected onto you by people who felt shameful themselves and tried to unburden themselves by displacing their sense of sin onto you. If you consider the hand motion associated with shaming someone, the dynamic is clear. Someone points an index finger at you with one hand (a symbol of judgment) and then rubs the index finger of the other hand against the first index finger, as if trying to slough off an unwanted object in your direction. It's as if someone has contracted filth and they are trying to flick it at you.

People who recognize their innocence do not need to shame others. Innocence sees innocence, and shame sees shame; such is the law of perception. A guilty world is the projection of guilty thoughts, and every guilty thought, whether projected inward or outward, underscores the illusion of shame. A loving world is the extension of loving thoughts. Every thought of gratitude reinforces the reality and presence of love.

If you feel shame, trace your experience back to the person(s) who put their shame on you, and recognize that you are the object not of the wrath of God, but the fear of man. Then realize that you are subject only to the love of God. Behold the end of shame.

> He was not born to shame.
> Upon his brow shame is ashamed to sit;
> For 'tis a throne where honor may be crowned
> Sole monarch of the universal earth.
> —William Shakespeare[2]

Saved from Wrath

When my mother was recovering from a surgery, she was in pain. She told me, "I must have done something really bad to deserve this." My heart broke to hear my mother say this. She was a wonderful woman who gave me extraordinary love and was very kind to everyone she knew. The idea of God punishing her was absurd to me. But to her it seemed real. I wish I could have taken a psychic scalpel and performed a shame-ectomy on her. I just told her she was wonderful, she didn't deserve pain, and I very much wanted her to feel better soon. I prayed for her by holding the vision of her as innocent, well, and whole.

Most people have been taught that pain is a punishment for sin. It is not. God does not want you or anyone to be in pain. Suffering is not the will of God. It is the result of distorted thinking. When you believe you are suffering for your sins or the sins of others, you but thicken illusion. When you break the assumed chain of causation between sin and punishment, you are ending the hypnosis that keeps the world in misery.

> We are forgiven now. And we are saved from all the wrath we thought belonged to God, and

> found it was a dream. We are restored to sanity, in which we understand that anger is insane, attack is mad, and vengeance merely foolish fantasy. We have been saved from wrath because we learned we were mistaken. Nothing more than that.
>
> —*A Course in Miracles*[3]

Mercy Justified

God does not want you to suffer any more than you want your children to suffer. When we love our children purely, we are most like God. When we demonstrate compassion for our children, we justify mercy.

My friend Jenny and her husband have adopted three Asian children. "Our five-year-old son was born without a right hand, and abandoned as a baby," she told me. "In China it is considered a stigma to be left-handed, so his parents left him on a street corner." How parents could abandon a child like that is appalling to me. Yet for every act of cruelty, the force of compassion comes to offset it. As dark and violent as life on the planet can be, the light of kindness redeems it. As we take care of each other, love establishes itself as the foundation of our reality. As English poet and politician Edward Bulwer-Lytton stated, "A good heart is better than all the heads in the world."

A New Way of Thinking

We are living in an extraordinary era when old limiting beliefs are falling away rapidly. During the recent epoch we have seen the end of slavery, the demise of monarchy, the fall of Communism, and the dissolution of

Apartheid. The United States has elected and re-elected its first African-American president. It may not be long before a woman takes that office. Considering that just under a hundred years ago women in this country were not allowed to vote, you can see how far we have come in a relatively short time within the big picture of evolution. In other arenas, child labor laws now protect children from exploitation, environmentalists have staved off extinction of many species, and public facilities are adapted for use by the disabled. While there still remain many forms of prejudice, unconsciousness, and mistreatment we must address and heal, the world is a more humane place than it was not very long ago.

One longstanding limiting belief that still must fall is the belief in the value of punishment. Inflicting pain on self or others runs counter to our nature as Godly beings. When you realize that you do not deserve punishment, you will not accept it from anyone else. Eleanor Roosevelt declared, "No one can make you feel inferior without your consent." We don't need to keep hurting ourselves. For the best experiment of your life, try letting yourself off the hook. You might be amazed to discover that it was but you who put yourself there. And it is you who takes yourself off.

We are all like the little Chinese boy who was abandoned by his parents because of his deformity. None of us is perfect as the world demands perfection; the world has an ugly propensity for rejection. But there exists a greater force that embraces us no matter our human inadequacies. Grace accepts where the world rejects. Grace honors where the world judges. Grace blesses where the world curses. The Force of Grace is the redemption of the world.

CHAPTER 8

Grace Beyond Belief

Do not believe in anything simply because you have heard it. Do not believe in anything simply because it is spoken and rumored by many or it is found written in your religious books. Do not believe in traditions because they have been handed down for many generations. But after observation and analysis, when you find that anything agrees with reason and is conducive to the good and benefit of one and all, then accept it and live up to it.

—attributed to Buddha

WHEN AYDEN BYLE MOVED into Toronto's Cedarvale neighborhood, he had a bright idea. Just for fun, he began to scribe inspiring thoughts on a chalkboard and post them in his living room window. "*One simple hello could change everything"* got passersby's attention. *"Is there any place better than here?"* moved them to think deeper. Soon neighbors and commuters were going out of their way to walk or drive past Ayden's window, hoping for an insight that might make their day more worthwhile.

One day a sign showed up in Ayden Byle's window that could make all the difference in a lifetime if the reader grasped its true message:

Grace trumps karma.

For most people, karma is not a happy word. Usually we associate it with bad karma, a payback or punishment for past misdeeds. I rarely hear people talking about their good karma. More often I hear, "My bad karma came back to me in the form of my ex." "Little children have diseases because of karma from a previous life." "It was just my karma to be driving past that speed trap and get a ticket." The Beatles' song warned that instant karma's gonna get you. Karma has become more of a villain in our lives than an ally.

How, then, does Grace trump karma? Is there some way that karma can be an *expression* of Grace, rather than its foe? Could *all* of our karma be good, even when it seems bad? Let's look at how this might be so.

Karma has nothing to do with punishment. It is a feedback mechanism, a cosmic GPS letting you know when you are on track with your well-being, and when you have veered from it. When "good karma" shows up, the universe is saying, "Right on, ____________________ [Fill in your name]. You are now in alignment with your purpose. Just keep headed in this direction and you will be cruising." When "bad karma" shows up, the universe is saying, "You have temporarily stepped away from your path of well-being. If you keep going in this direction, it will hurt.

Here is your sign that it's time to do something different so you can return to your soul's purpose and be happy." In this sense, *all* karma is a gift and a blessing.

Karma is a mirror reflecting the information you need in order to succeed. Imagine you are about to go on a big date or deliver an important presentation to a large audience. Just before your date or the presentation, you look in the mirror and discover a huge piece of spinach protruding from between your two front teeth. Wouldn't you be grateful for the reflection the mirror gave you? The reflection says nothing about sin, punishment, or how good or a bad person you are. It is an entirely neutral device providing you with information to help you. Just as you would be grateful to the mirror, you can be grateful to your karma, including the reflection of how nice your hair looks, along with your teeth.

In this sense, karma *is* Grace. The key, then, to changing, offsetting, or improving your karma, is to appreciate karma as Grace and change your interpretation of events so you see them as working in your favor. What if your evil ex is really an angel who came to help you dig deeper into your soul to remember who you are, speak your truth, choose love over fear, and make healthier relationship choices? What if children with diseases open our hearts, deepen our compassion, and help us to recognize the angels they are? Or to watch miracles unfold as they heal? What if your speeding ticket motivates you to slow down, take better care of yourself, and enjoy the ride as much as getting to your destination? Or your DUI or driver's license suspension pushes you to recognize how dangerously you have been living, and sober up?

Just as we have twisted karma to seem a dark force, we can spin it to be a light force. Karma is the opening act that sets the stage for Grace to complete the play. "For God had not given us the spirit of fear; but of power, and of love, and of a sound mind."[1] Any burdensome situation is not over until Grace has had the final word. Grace *is* the final word.

The Law of Attraction 2.0

The Law of Attraction, the principle that the thoughts and beliefs you dwell on draw unto you events and experiences of like nature, is always working on your behalf. Used wisely, it can progress your life in powerful ways. When limited thinking gets a hold of it, however, it becomes a tool of the Law of Distraction. Let's look at how you can bypass struggling with the Law of Attraction and incorporate it into a broader vision that embraces the Law of Grace.

People misunderstand and misuse the Law of Attraction in three ways. First, they believe they have to huff, puff, sweat, and hustle to get their thoughts up to speed to work their way into the vortex of success. The goal is correct, but the method is faulty. Certainly as you think more positively, you will attract better results. But *anxiously striving* to master the Law of Attraction offsets the results you seek to achieve. Struggling to achieve *anything* runs counter to the truth that your good arrives by virtue of joy, not pain. The more relaxed and more confident you are that the universe will deliver your good, the faster and more efficiently it will show up. The "trying" part is the most trying part. The more you ease up and flow, the more readily your blessings will find you.

The second way people misuse the Law of Attraction is as an excuse to beat themselves up. "My soulmate has not shown up because I polluted my vortex with negative thoughts," for example. The dynamic may be true, but *how you view* the dynamic determines the experience you generate. If you feel like a failure for not attracting your goal, your self-definition as a sinner, oaf, or loser is keeping you out of the vortex of positive creation. You are never more than one thought away from getting back into your right mind. What if, instead, you gave yourself credit for your efforts to find your soulmate? What if you blessed the positive attributes of the people you have dated, and what you learned from those experiences, rather than cursing them because they didn't turn out to be "The One?" What if you trusted the Law of Grace to help you connect with a wonderful partner rather than having to shake your good out of the universe like rattling a soda machine to dislodge a can of pop? There is more to life than impersonal scientific principles. You are loved more deeply than is indicated by the sterile formulas to which you have ascribed your power. Kindness to yourself—an act of Grace—will get you back into your creative zone far more rapidly than using science to bludgeon your innocence.

The third way people misuse the Law of Attraction is to attempt to micromanage the results; to specify what and how and when your good should arrive. "I want my new job with Hewlett-Packard by next Monday." But are you so sure that working at HP is in your best interests? What if there is an even better opportunity for you? Might there be other more important things for you to be doing by Monday? Maybe you would do better to enjoy more time renewing yourself before you dive back into the corporate arena. Perhaps that entrepreneurial idea you have been nurturing would net you more joy and success in the long run. Perhaps you might go instead to Starbucks on Monday and there meet someone who offers you a position that exceeds your wildest dreams. Rather than trying to force your good, you do better to affirm, "I am always supported by the universe to have all I want and need, and I trust that I will be matched with the perfect job for me in the perfect way and timing." If it's HP by Monday, there you will be. If there is a better place and time, there you will be. How easy can it get?

The Law of Attraction functions at a level far deeper than your conscious thoughts. Your thoughts are important, but *the intentions of your soul* are more important. Your soul signature, the energetic matrix of your inner being, is broadcasting intentions that attract far more than your surface thoughts attract. The key is to trust and allow your authentic self to magnetize what is truly yours. Your good is hurtling at light speed to find its way to you. All that is not a match to you is clawing at the cage door to flee from you. Your role is to stand confidently in your true self, let your good in, and let your bad go. The universe knows precisely how to orchestrate right comings and goings without you bossing the process. The best things that happen are unplanned by the conscious mind. You cannot afford to put the ego in charge of the Law of Attraction. Let the Law of Grace, functioning *through* the Law of Attraction, work its magic on your behalf.

While the universe is based on scientific principles, it is more fundamentally ruled by love. Albert Einstein, one of the most brilliant scientists of all time, was a deeply spiritual man. He said, "Love is a better teacher than duty," and "How on earth are you ever going to explain in terms of chemistry and physics so important a biological phenomenon as first love?" Science is ultimately spiritual, and spirituality is ultimately scientific. As one philosopher quipped, "When the scientists finally arrive at the top of the mountain of truth, there they will find the theologians laughing like hell."

The Religion of Radiance

Religion is empowering only to the extent that it teaches Grace. Religions, to a large extent, have fixated on sin and punishment, which obscure Grace. The purpose of religion is to affirm the presence of love. If your religion doesn't find love right where you stand, in you, as you, around you, and for you, it is missing the point. A healthy religion leads you to experience deep wholeness, connects you with an all-forgiving God, and makes you happier to be alive. If your religion makes you feel guilty, afraid, or outside of love's reach; calls you to suffer; or threatens you with hell; the devil has hijacked the faith. When you go to church, synagogue, mosque, or the sweat lodge, you should feel more joyful and less alone. Any implied sense of deficiency, debt, or incompetence has nothing to do with healing. Your soul is eternally whole and spiritually solvent.

While religion was intended to connect us with God, (the word "religion" means "to unite") it is often used to separate us from God. Some religions inculcate elitism: "The only way to get saved is to be one of us." The voice of insecurity has never spoken louder. If your minister tells you that those in your flock are the only ones going to heaven, run out the door as fast as you can. All people are equally holy, loveable, and valuable in the eyes of God. God does not care what religion you are. God cares that you are happy and that you recognize your identity as a divine being. All else is detail. The form in which you worship is less important than the heart you bring to the altar. God's altar is not branded. If you live with love in your heart, you are doing God's will. And if you don't live with love in your heart, you are loved anyway. You have just missed the memo.

Your purpose is not to convert sinners. Your purpose is to convert your consciousness. The ego projects sin onto the outer world to avoid facing the belief in sin in oneself. Then you try to fix other people to compensate for your perceived insufficiency. Proselytization is motivated by lack of self-knowledge. Those secure in their own beliefs do not need to corral others to join them. If your faith is strong, you will inspire and attract those seeking the light, and help them more by your model than your preaching. Joseph Campbell put it eloquently: "Preachers err by trying to talk people into belief—better they reveal the radiance of their own discovery."

Go to church if you feel so moved, or find church wherever you are. Everywhere you are, God is. Inspiring sermons are being articulated and stirring hymns are being sung to you with every encounter. Your Higher Power does not live in one building. The entire universe is the temple of God.

Real Self-Help

After many years as a student, writer, and teacher in the self-help movement, I realize that ultimately we cannot help ourselves. The you that is trying to help yourself is the you that needs help. *A Course in Miracles* tells us, "You cannot be your guide to miracles for it is you that made them necessary."[2] All of your problems issue from the notion that you are frail, lacking, limited, powerless, and victimized, at the mercy of people and forces stronger than you. When you proceed from that identity, there is no way you can succeed. Your small self has no idea how to run your life. If it did, your life would be working a lot better. Your only hope of healing is to connect with and live from a Self greater than the self you have been taught you are.

Twelve-step groups like Alcoholics Anonymous make wise use of this principle. Members affirm that their lives have become unmanageable and they needed to turn to a Higher Power for healing. We all have at least some portion of our life that feels unmanageable. That's because we have been trying to manage it from ego. If we would invite Higher Power to take over that piece of our life, it would work magnificently.

If you cut your finger, a deep innate wisdom will brilliantly mend it for you. You have no idea how to heal your finger. But your body, imbued with intelligence far beyond what you can conceive, knows exactly what to do. Even if you are a doctor and you understand the mechanics of healing, the process is guided by a Power greater than you. The best doctors stand in awe of nature and feel honored to participate in the healing process. My dentist's surgery professor told his class, "Don't worry too much about messing up doing surgery. The body has a brilliant capacity to heal itself." While this advice may be unsettling if you are on your way to surgery, it is ultimately soothing. You don't have to tell healing how to happen. You simply have to quit doing what is preventing healing from happening, and cooperate with nature. (Voltaire said, "the art of medicine consists in amusing the patient while nature cures the disease.") You must correct habits of thought, feeling, and action that run counter to your natural state of wellness. Then your body and your life will function like a well-oiled machine. Medicine can correct imbalances, but to sustain healing, you must maintain balance. Team with the Universal Physician, as you would by keeping a cut clean, bandaging it, and protecting it from further injury. Then healing will occur as the most natural experience in the world.

The best self-help books and teachings guide students to Higher Self. Those that do not, leave students hungry. Do what you can to help yourself, and meanwhile recognize that your true Source of help is God. Grace has you covered. If you have a favorite self-help practice, diet, or teacher, regard these methods as agents of the divine and use them. Higher awareness does not wish to yank your chosen tools from you. It would have you bless them and make positive use of them as long as they serve you. Ultimately you will find that you don't need any method. Grace will take you all the way home, through methods at first, and then beyond them all.

I am sustained by the Love of God.
—*A Course in Miracles*[3]

All belief systems exist to be transcended. Everything you now believe, one day you won't. You will find progressively larger cups to hold your life until one day the water you once held in a cup will become the ocean. Every belief system you employ is not a final destination, but a step toward it. A Zen maxim advises, "Do not mistake the finger pointing at the moon, for the moon itself." All methods are fingers pointing at healing. Grace is the fountain from which all healing springs. Probe, challenge, and grow beyond any belief system that does not acknowledge you as already divine and Grace as already present. Don't stop until everything you seek is already given.

CHAPTER 9

God is my Agent

"GET UP AND WRITE," the voice spoke to me. Lying in bed, half-awake, I rolled over and pulled the pillow over my head, hoping the half-asleep part would win.

"Get up and write," the voice repeated more emphatically. It was not the voice of a person in words. It was an intense urging.

I rolled over again and stuffed the pillow over the other ear.

"Listen clearly now," the voice went on: "Get up and write."

I sat up and looked around the room. No one was there. "I don't want to write," I retorted.

"That wasn't one of the questions."

"Okay, okay." I threw off the covers and shuffled, pajama-clad, to my little wooden desk next to the attic window of the house where I was renting a room. Bleary-eyed, I pulled a notebook and pen from the desk drawer and stared into space. "Now what?"

"Just start."

Befuddled, I began to jot down ideas on subjects I was most interested in: life, love, relationships, happiness, courage, and spirit. That seemed like a good place to start.

An hour later I had a few pages. I held up the notebook and looked at it as if it would explain itself to me. It didn't. I figured I was writing some notes for a talk I was to give at the end of the weekly yoga class I was teaching. I tossed the notebook on the desk and went back to bed.

But the urging didn't stop. As I stared at the ceiling, more ideas flooded my brain. I began to see relationships between big spiritual concepts and my life. Experiences long buried in my memory surfaced and arranged themselves in meaningful patterns. My soul's journey was starting to make sense. I understood how seemingly random and anomalous events fit into the empty jigsaw puzzle spaces of my life. Some cosmic muse was connecting the dots of everything that had ever happened to me. I was being shown the blueprint for my existence.

I went back to the desk. This writing, whatever it was, had a life of its own. I was not writing it. It was writing me.

Later that day I borrowed a typewriter and began to pound away, trying to keep up with the torrid pace of ideas streaming into my brain. This process went on day and night, twelve, fifteen, eighteen hours a day. The Presence behind the current of thought, whatever it was, was bigger than me. I stopped only to eat, sleep, and jog. One day I ran seven miles in the park. I needed that physical exertion to balance the intense mental work I was doing.

After a few weeks I realized that a book was begging me for birth. I'd read lots of books, but never written one. This one was my book, my baby, my creation. It was the closest experience I have ever had to what I imagine it must be like for a woman to give birth. Less painful, for sure—but for me, equally meaningful.

A friend gave me a recording of the Paul Winter Consort album, *Common Ground*. One song, *Lay Down Your Burden*, angelically sung by Susan Osborn, culminated in a haunting refrain: *The Dragon Doesn't Live Here Anymore*. I played the song over and over and over, until I was nearly in tears. I was being given the title.

But what good is a book if no one can read it? I sent the manuscript to a half-dozen publishers. They all went thumbs down. One publisher asked me, "What's the book about?"

"The healing power of love and forgiveness."

"Naah," he snarled. "Write something more dynamic."

Huh?

Eventually I found the courage to tell my mother I had written a book.

"What's it about?"

"Love, truth, and healing."

"You're nuts!"

Maybe she's not the one to tell about the book.

The next day my mother phoned me. "Would you like the money publish it?"

Normally I wouldn't have taken my mother's money. She had only five thousand dollars in the world, her life savings, stashed in a safe deposit box. "You're going to get it when I die," she told me as she placed the cash in my hand. "You might as well use it now."

I found a printer and made a deal to print a thousand books. I went to the company's office, met their rep, and signed the contract. As I placed my hand on the doorknob to exit his office, he called to me, "You know, they say that you don't make any money until your third book."

Well, thanks for chucking a psychic bowling ball into my gut. Not the kind of thing you want to hear after you've worked your tail off for a year and invested your mother's life savings into a visionary project. I turned, faced the agent, and these words came out of my mouth:

"I know that's what they might say . . . but what they may not know is that my agent is God."

I wasn't trying to be a smartass. Those were the only words I knew how to say. I had to uphold my work rather than letting it fall prey to the vultures of limiting beliefs.

The agent just stared at me. He had no response. I didn't need one. I needed to say those words more than he needed to hear them.

A few months later I held my precious book, my child, in my hands. What started out as a tiny seed idea was now a real, tangible, living thing. I invited all of my friends to a launch party at my house, where we prayed that the book would touch and uplift its readers. The next day I took a case of books to a local bookstore and asked the owner if he would sell some. "I'll take fifty," he said. Now, years later, I realize that was a lot of books for him to buy up front.

A few weeks later I was passing by the bookstore and stopped in to see if any of the books had sold. "We've been trying to contact you," the girl behind the counter told me. "Your books have sold out. We want to order more."

Really?

Then I received in the mail the brochure of a distributor of inspirational books. I thought about asking the company to sell my books, but being ignorant about business and shy to promote myself, I tossed the brochure in the trash. The next day I received a letter from a friend, containing a copy of the exact brochure I had trashed. She wrote, "I think you should send your book to these people." *Okay, okay, how many signs do I need?* The distributor was eager to take my book and disseminate it nationwide. Before long they were sending me checks for $10,000 a month.

I took my mother back to her safe deposit box at the bank, the very place from which she had drawn her life savings to invest in her son's nutty project. I opened the box and showed her that the $5,000 in cash was back, and then some. Her eyes bulged.

I placed the cash in her hands. "Thank you for believing in me, mom."

She smiled and handed me back the money. "You keep it. Do with it as you like."

Years later a New York publisher purchased the book with a sizeable advance that enabled me to take a year off, hire a business manager, and purchase a property in Hawaii. Now, over thirty years later, the book is still in print, selling at a regular clip.

Looking back now, I realize that when I told the publisher, "God is my agent," I had only the faintest idea of the truth behind that statement.

What Spirit Wants

God is your agent, too, if you are open and willing to accept divine representation. Any project that sends the chemistry of passion coursing through your body and soul is Spirit-guided. Higher Power has already signed on the dotted line, but you must agree to enjoy its benefits. Yet we get distracted by limiting beliefs, opinions, and pressures, and we believe we must do it all ourselves. *We don't*. We must do what we can, while trusting and allowing a larger hand to orchestrate our destiny.

A friend of mine, eager to get her book published, went to a publishing convention where she attended a panel discussion by top inspirational authors. The writers went into daunting detail about all the requirements for a new author to be published. As prerequisite piled upon prerequisite and the number of hoops she would have to jump through added up to a seemingly impossible degree, my friend grew quite discouraged. "I'll never be able to do all these things they are telling me I need to do!" she thought, and started to leave the room.

Then the microphone went to panel member Clarissa Pinkola Estés, author of the wildly popular *Women Who Run with the Wolves*. Her comment was brief: "If Spirit wants your book published, it will be published."

If Spirit wants *anything* done, it will happen, no matter the false prerequisites the human mind lays over divine possibilities. The will of God is unbendable and unbreakable. You have a soul contract with success according to your unique calling. Do your part, and let Spirit do Its part.

An agent is someone who believes in you, represents you better than you can represent yourself, and organizes connections and events to maximize your success. Many human agents perform such tasks, but ultimately, at best, they serve as vessels through which a Higher Agent impeccably organizes all events in harmony with your best interest and that of those you serve.

If you are seeking a mate; harmony in a relationship; a job; a home; healing; success for your creative project; right direction for your children; the answer to an important question; a vision for your life—you don't have to do it all yourself. You *can't* do it all yourself. Get yourself a good agent. You *already* have the best Agent you could ever want, but you must let that Agent work on your behalf.

It takes humility to say, "I need help," but such a request is *always heard and answered.* At this moment you have access to help from above. When you summon it, it is yours. If your child came to you with a sincere need, you would not hesitate to do all you could to fulfill that child's need. If, as worldly parents, our dedication to our children is so strong, how much greater is our Divine Parent's willingness to help us when we really need it?

Listen to the panel on how things get done, but remember how things really get done.

Much of life appears mundane at the time. Yet in God's providence every moment includes significant details arranged by His divine hand.

—Dillon Burroughs

CHAPTER 10

Who Walks with You

"I NEARLY FELL TO MY DEATH on a rock climb," my coaching client Bill told me. "While my buddy and I were crossing a ravine, I slipped and fell 25 feet until I was hanging perilously over a deep canyon. I called to my partner for help. He made a few strides down, but then he became frightened and ventured no further. Just then I noticed a rock I could grab onto, which stabilized me. From that place I spied another rock, and then another, which I clutched until I worked my way back to safety. Since that day I have harbored tremendous anger at God for abandoning me when my friend chickened out. How could any loving God be so callous?"

"God did not desert you," I told Bill.

"How is that?"

"God showed you the rock that gave you a foothold to make your way to safety."

You may be tempted to see yourself as deprived, betrayed, lost, or without resource. You may feel that God does not know you, or if He did, He has abandoned you. *It is not so.* Only when obscured by clouds of illusion could God seem absent. When you understand that unseen forces are caring for you with impeccable ingenuity, you will rest in a security the world cannot provide. *A Course in Miracles* reassures us:

If you knew Who walks beside you on the way that you have chosen, fear would be impossible.[1]

The Course urges us to ask many times daily, *"Who walks with me?"*[2] Put in other words:

"Is there a benevolent consciousness that cares about me and provides for me and my loved ones?"

"Do I have access to wisdom that will show me exactly what to do to resolve this situation in favor of all concerned?"

"Do I have angels, guides, and mentors who whisper to my soul at key crossroads, and orchestrate events on my behalf?"

Such questions, asked sincerely, will always yield positive answers. Perhaps not in the moment or form you demand them, but come they will. Every great artist, inventor, teacher, healer, and conscious leader acknowledges inspiration from a source that transcends the world. Mozart declared, "It is when I am, as it were, completely myself, entirely alone, and of good cheer . . . that ideas flow best and most abundantly. Whence and how they come, I know not, nor can I force them." Thoreau echoed, "I believe that there is a subtle magnetism in Nature, which if we unconsciously yield to it, will direct us aright." Einstein put it this way: "The intuitive mind is a sacred gift and the rational mind is a faithful servant."

Don't Boss the Form

You may have your idea about how your good is supposed to come, and when. But if you are fixated on results showing up in the way and time you designate, you might miss even better avenues through which Providence can reach you. Perhaps the partner you thought was the one for you turned out to be unavailable, unfaithful, or have a tragic flaw. Or you could not get financing for the house you were sure was right for you. Or the business deal you were counting on fell through. A sense of struggle, frustration, or disappointment is a sign that you are trying to force something not in harmony with your best interest. At such a time, assume that something else better is trying to find you, and it will. You are not hitting a dead end. You are being redirected.

A young woman phoned in to my radio show and complained that the fellow she had a crush on had rejected her. "He told me not to phone or text him, and I am so disappointed," she reported.

"Why would you want to pursue someone who doesn't want you?" I asked her. "This fellow obviously doesn't recognize the beauty and value you offer. Or he is simply not a good match for you. I assure you that there is someone else out there who will desire and appreciate you for who you are. If you are busy chasing someone who doesn't care, you are not available to someone who *does* care. Let go of what doesn't fit so you are free to receive what does fit."

Be sure not to confuse *avenues* of Providence with the

Source of Providence. You may believe that a person is the Source, and attribute undo authority to that person. Then you may become anxious if that person is not performing according to your expectations. You can avoid such disappointment by recognizing the difference between the *gift* and the *messenger*. Build a relationship with the factory rather than the delivery truck.

We confuse avenue with Source when we believe our well-being depends on the boss approving of us; our ex keeping up with alimony payments; the government providing benefits; a doctor giving us a clean bill of health; a priest forgiving us; a therapist guiding us correctly; a contractor following through on a job; a friend being loyal to us; and so on. While such blessings can certainly come through such vehicles, our good is not limited to them or dependent on them. If one ascribed source does not show up, dries up, or disappears, there are many more ways you can be taken care of. The avenues through which providence can arrive are infinite. Take back the power you have attributed to a particular person or entity, and you will find that the stream of abundance, health, and love can and will arrive through another venue.

When you knock, ask to see God—none of the servants.

—Henry David Thoreau

You are not required to bang down doors to love or success. The right doors will open in the right way and time, like a department store door opens automatically when you enter the field within the scope of its electric eye. What you seek is seeking you and will find you. The universe functions in perfect complementary balance. For every need you have, there is someone or something out there seeking you or what you have to offer. I saw a clever billboard ad for a sexy car. The tag line: *It wants you, too*.

The Provider

"I lost my job and now I am not able to provide for my family," a fellow reported at a seminar during an economic recession. "I feel like a failure, less than a man."

I replied, "You are missing one important point which, if you understand it, will bring you great comfort."

"What's that?"

"You are not the Provider," I told him as I wrote the word *Provider* on a whiteboard, emphasizing the upper case "P." "You are the *provider*," I explained, scribing the word with the lower case "p."

"You are a conduit, one of many possible avenues, through which Providence can flow to you and your family. The idea that you are the *sole* provider is born of ego. You are attempting to usurp the role of God, an impossible supposition that inevitably leads to confusion, despair, and depression."

The fellow tried to absorb the idea.

"Can you imagine any other way your family can be provided for?" I asked.

"Well, my wife said she would be willing to work during this time to help our income."

"So you see there are other ways—many ways, really—that your family can be taken care of," I told him. "Certainly do your part and make your best effort to keep sustenance flowing. But ultimately it's not *all* up to you. You are sustained by a Hand far greater than your own."

If you feel overwhelmed by responsibilities to take care of yourself or others, remember that you are an *aspect* of God, but you are not *all* of God. You may feel that the world rests upon your shoulders, and unless you perform impeccably, all will be lost. You may believe you are the only source of another person's happiness; that their well-being is your success, and their distress represents your failure. If so, remember that you are but one character in the divine play. You must play your part, but you cannot play all the parts. You have been assigned your lines, and God has not forgotten His.

Contact the Director

When I moved my office to a rural location in Hawaii, we requested several telephone lines to be installed. To my disappointment, the telephone company told my office manager that because the phone company infrastructure in that area was antiquated and limited, only one line was available. That wouldn't quite do, since we needed at least two lines. My manager, a very determined and efficient guy, vigorously pursued the issue with the phone company. After a week he told me, "I've worked my way up the food chain at the phone company, and everyone has said 'no.' I am now on a first-name basis with the phone company's Director of Consumer Affairs, who has told me firmly there is no way to get more than one line."

I told him, "Then let's call on the real Director. Let's pray about this and see if we can get help from beyond the phone company." We said a prayer together and let the issue go.

When the phone installer came, we told him we needed more than one line. "I'll see what I can do," he told us. An hour later he returned from the phone pole and told us, "You have your two lines."

People do not have the final word. God does. When you ask sincerely, your "yes" can come through surprising and wondrous channels.

Who was Driving?

One day I was driving with a friend on a winding road through a valley. We were absorbed in a fascinating conversation. When we reached the other side of the valley I had no recollection of driving for the last few minutes, or anything I had seen or heard during that time, except for the content of our conversation. If you had asked me to describe what was beside the road, or what car I was following, or what speed I was driving, I could not. *Who, then, was driving?* I was sitting in the driver's seat; steering the wheel; keeping the car in the proper lane at a healthy distance behind the car in front of me; braking when necessary; performing all the functions of driving—but since I was paying no conscious attention to any of these activities, there was obviously an intelligence that took over when my mind was elsewhere.

When you consider the trillions of microscopic biological processes that operate every moment to keep your body alive and healthy—your heart beats; your lungs breathe; your brain fires billions of tiny neurological impulses; your stomach digests; your kidneys purify; hormones enable your reproductive system; and on and on and on—it is ludicrous to think that you are in charge of this myriad of functions. You have no idea how to beat your heart or fire neurons in your brain. All of these processes are being managed for you automatically, beyond your conscious control, so you can focus on other tasks at hand. Who, then, walks with you? And Who, then, walks *as* you?

From Supernatural to Super Natural

When spiritual teacher Ram Dass[3] went to India on a quest for enlightenment, his life was transformed when he met his guru, Neem Karoli Baba, also known as Maharaj-ji. This enlightened master showed Ram Dass extraordinary love, wisdom, and power that moved Ram Dass to devote his life to spiritual awakening. Before Ram Dass returned to America, Maharaj-ji told him not to tell anyone about him. Yet Ram Dass, in his exuberance, told lots of people, and a few years later he returned to India to see his guru, followed by a large group who wanted to sit in the master's presence.

Since Maharaj-ji lived a very unpredictable lifestyle, spontaneously moving from town to town and temple to temple, it was difficult to know where he would be and when. One had to just show up and hope the guru might be there.

One day Ram Dass and his entourage of 23 aspirants took a private bus to Delhi to buy food. Along the way someone suggested the group visit the grounds of the Kumbh Mela, a spiritual festival that a hundred million Indians attend annually. The festival had finished a week earlier, but the group decided to go anyway.

As the bus pulled into the fairgrounds, someone spotted Maharaj-ji. Thrilled, the group flocked off the bus to meet him. He told everyone to follow him to the place where he was staying. When the group entered the house, the woman who lived there led them to a dining table where 25 meal settings had been prepared—the precise number of people on the bus, including the bus driver. When the astonished guests asked the hostess how she knew to set the meal up, she explained, "Maharaj-ji woke me up at six o'clock in the morning and told me to have lunch ready for 25 guests."

Such events might be called supernatural, but from a higher perspective they are *super natural.* An advanced soul like Maharaj-ji lives in attunement with the Mind of God, so the will of God is done easily through such a person. Maharaj-ji would be the first to admit that he and spiritual masters like him are not privy to a unique connection with the Mind of God. Such gifts are available to all of us when we put aside the chatter of the "monkey mind" and let higher wisdom flow to us and through us. This story bears an even deeper teaching in that Maharaj-ji demonstrated Grace in providing so generously for the guests even after Ram Dass had disobeyed his guru's order not to publicize him.

The Guru in Your iPod

Visionary innovator Steven Jobs was also a student of Maharaj-ji. As a young man, Jobs was deeply influenced by Ram Dass's book *Be Here Now*,[4] and he went to India to meet Maharaj-ji. By that time the guru had passed on, but Jobs kept the master in his heart as a source of inspiration throughout his life. I am told that Jobs had a photo of Maharaj-ji in his room at the time of his death.

Actress Julia Roberts has more recently been touched by this guru, many years after his physical passing. While Roberts was in India filming *Eat, Pray, Love*, she came across a photo of Maharaj-ji, which affected her profoundly by the energy she felt emanating from it. Upon exploring Maharaj-ji and his teachings, Roberts became a Hindu, gave her children Hindu names, and now attends a Hindu temple.

I find it fascinating that this little old man who usually wore nothing but a blanket, and who wandered through remote villages in India, has transformed the lives of many millions of people, initially through *Be Here Now,* and eventually through many other notable individuals. As a result of Maharaj-ji's inspirational effect on Steven Jobs, one of the most technologically influential geniuses of the modern age, we might say that Maharaj-ji has indirectly contributed to all the phenomenal inventions birthed through Jobs, including Apple Computers, Pixar Animation Studios, the iPod, iPhone, iPad, and many related devices. If you use any Apple product or are affected by someone who uses one—that adds up to all of us—you can thank, in part, a small naked guru who never saw a computer in his life, but whose Grace gave life to billions of them.

At this moment One walks with you and knows you and what you need. You do not have to talk God into helping you. You have to talk yourself into receiving the gifts already given, and those to come. You have a spiritual escrow account into which vast sustenance has been deposited on your behalf. You do not have to add to that account. You need but draw from it. "God has already done all things that need be done."[5] You are called to claim your inheritance, which is infinite, sustainable, and not rescindable. You deserve it not because you have earned it, or you will. You deserve it because you exist as God's great idea.

"Who walks with me?" Ask this question a thousand times a day and you will receive a thousand affirmations that you do not walk alone. God has no orphans. An invisible hand guides you at every turn, firms you when you falter, and delivers your infinite good. Greater love no one has ever known.

CHAPTER 11

The Ease Factor

I come into the peace of wild things who do not
tax their lives with forethought of grief. . .
For a time I rest in the grace of the world,
and am free.

—Wendell Berry

FOR SOME ODD REASON, many of us believe that if we're not struggling, we're not doing it correctly. A friend told me, "I can turn anything into boot camp." If you have been struggling for many years or most of your life, you may wonder if all the angst is really necessary. *It's not.*

Grace asks you to believe that your life can be easy. If that vision seems too hard to believe, begin by considering the possibility that your life could at least be easier. Freedom from struggle might seem like a bold assertion, considering the value of anxious striving that you have been taught, the nobility you have been trained to associate with sacrifice, the martyrs you have observed and even taken as role models, and the hardship you have experienced. But it may be precisely the insight you need to get out of hell. Are you willing to reconsider the struggle ethic and open to ease as a more practical success tool than strife?

When We'll All Get There

I live on a country road that gets so skinny at some points that only one car can pass. When two cars meet, one must back up or pull off the road to make way for the other. While the process is inconvenient, it calls for cooperation and saying hi to neighbors. It's refreshing.

One day I was on my way to an important meeting I did not want to be late for. At one of the thin junctures I encountered my neighbor Dean approaching in his truck. The moment came when we had to decide which vehicle would yield. While normally I wouldn't have minded backing up, that day I wished I didn't have to. Dean seemed to read my mind and he congenially reversed his truck quite a distance to let me pass. When I passed him I rolled down my window to say thanks. "No problem," he smiled. "We'll all get where we need to get when we need to get there."

Now there's an affirmation worthy of posting on a huge screen inside your forehead! Many of us spend a great deal of our life hustling to get places. In the process we do clumsy things, grow irritated and impatient, sometimes cause accidents, and make mistakes that cost us twice the time and hassle than if we had taken our time in the first place. In our haste to get somewhere, we miss *being* somewhere, and never seem to get anywhere. When you realize that being present is more fulfilling than getting somewhere, the ride becomes as rewarding as the destination.

Are you Having Fun, Honey?

My partner Dee and I support each other to choose joy. If one of us sees the other struggling, we call it to the other person's attention and invite her or him to refocus on well-being. Serving as a mirror for a partner is one of the most empowering elements of a healthy relationship.

One evening I was sitting at my computer trying to rectify an error on my website. Without realizing it, I had gotten balled up in the technical intricacies, and I had become an unhappy camper. At that moment Dee passed through the room and noticed I was struggling. "Are you having fun, honey?" she asked me.

I looked up with a sour face. "Not really."

"Then stop," she said in a soft but authoritative voice, and went on her way.

Fortunately I had the presence of mind to take her advice. I walked away from the computer and turned to another activity. The next morning I revisited the website issue from a fresh perspective, and handled it quickly.

You have been taught that when you have a problem, the way to solve it is to push harder and fight more until you buck through it and subdue it, like roping an ornery calf in a rodeo. While this method can work—basically because you believe it will—there are easier ways to get the job done.

When facing a challenging situation, you will find your solution more gracefully by stepping back, breathing, clearing your mind, calming your emotions, renewing yourself, and approaching the state of affairs from a more expanded perspective. The problem is calling you not to work harder, but to work smarter. If something you are doing is not working, doing more of it will not work better. To underscore a principle mentioned earlier, what you perceive as a dead end sign is really an arrow pointing you in another direction. Metaphysically speaking, no road really ends; it simply gives way to a more productive route. Nothing stops without something else beginning.

Danielle LaPorte, author of *Fire Starter Sessions*[1], brilliantly advises, "Quit trying to be good at what makes you feel bad." If something you are doing is obnoxious to your soul, you cannot afford to continue. Ask yourself what, by contrast, would be *nourishing* to your soul, and head in that direction. You will be amazed at the avenues that present themselves, the people and events you attract, and the success that accrues when your actions are lined up with your spirit. Projects founded in passion take off like a rocket ship. Projects devoid of passion fall off the gantry and go *thud*. When an enterprise is flowing naturally, you have a sign that you are headed in the right direction. When life becomes an uphill climb, you have veered from your purpose. Are you having fun, honey?

This is not to say that worthwhile projects do not present challenges. Setting your sights on a lofty goal often calls forth adverse reaction from within you and around you. But if your excitement, vision, and sense of intention are greater than the challenges, you will be motivated to overcome them, and you will. The fire of purpose consumes and transforms all obstacles in its path. Joy is the fuel for the fire of purpose. When you love what you do, fear cannot stop you.

If there is something you must do that you would rather not do, find a way to hold it that does not deplete you. The reason it feels like work is *resistance*. So if you must do something you find distasteful, do your best to drop resistance. Remind yourself why you are choosing to do this, and keep your head in a positive zone. When you release resistance, the endeavor will go faster and easier, and you will come out on the other side. Even more important, you will have kept your soul alive.

If it's not Fun, Hire it Done

One of the most common difficulties I hear about from my coaching clients, especially those of artistic nature, is that they do not know how to manage a business, nor do they want to. "I would rather just create my crafts, connect with clients, and keep innovating," I typically hear. "I shrivel when I think about bookkeeping, maintaining a website, or promoting myself."

I tell such clients, "If it's not fun, hire it done."

Not everyone is good at everything, nor are you supposed to be. Artists generally do not enjoy or do well at spreadsheets, and computer programmers rarely have easels in their living room. Most people are either logical left-brain dominant, or artistic right-brain dominant. It's rare that broad-stroke vision and detailed execution share real estate in one head.

That's fine. You do not need to force yourself to become someone you are not. The key is to make the best use of your unique talents and inclinations while teaming with others who are making the best use of theirs. I tell artists, "Hire someone to do what you do not want to do or cannot do. There are people out there whose idea of heaven is creating a marketing plan. Give such a person an opportunity to shine while they support you to shine. The right person will help you earn enough to pay them, while expanding your income. If you don't have the capital to pay someone at the outset, strike a percentage deal with them, barter, or make another creative arrangement. As your shared venture grows, you will both profit. There's a place in the sun for everyone."

If you feel burdened by aspects of your business venture that you would rather not do, take a piece of paper and create two columns, *For Me* and *For Someone Else*. In the *For Me* column, list all the elements of your job that you enjoy doing and that are working for you. In the *For Someone Else* column, record all the elements you don't enjoy and are not working. Then tear the paper into two pieces. The *For Me* paper is your job description. The *For Someone Else* paper is someone else's job description. Here you have a short course in successful entrepreneurship.

You will succeed at doing what you love far more gloriously than you will succeed at doing what you don't love. This simple recognition, and the actions that proceed from it, will change *everything*.

Lightheart

The ancient Egyptians believed that when a person died, he or she would meet the god Anubis, who would weigh the person's heart against a feather. If the heart was as light as a feather, the person would be allowed to enter heaven. If not, the demon god Ammit would come and devour the heart, and the soul would wander unfulfilled for eternity.

This metaphor applies more to life than afterlife. When your heart is light, you enter the kingdom of heaven, even as you walk the earth. You are *already* entitled to the kingdom of heaven, but if you are immersed in the tyranny of triviality, you will not recognize the blessings already given. Our earthly journey is not about getting anything. It is about waking up to what we already have.

If your heart is not as light as a feather, the muck and mire of fear, conflict, and anxious effort will devour your peace. The Law of Grace keeps you from truly being devoured, because as a divine being you are undevourable. But you can have the *experience* of feeling devoured or vulnerable to being devoured, which is not high on the list of the top ten desirable experiences. So you don't need to poke yourself into your vortex with a cattle prod. You just need to lighten up.

Ease is the secret path to success. It is secret not because it is hidden, but because so few people recognize it and make use of it. If struggle led to happiness, we would all be in ecstasy by now. But struggle only reinforces itself and perpetuates the same experience. It takes courage to trust ease, because so many people don't. Conscious ease does not imply laziness. Work, activity, action, and perseverance may be required. But "a labor of love is no labor at all."

Self-brutality, burdensome obligation, threat, pretense, and unspoken dissatisfaction have no place in a healthy work environment, relationship, or life. If you are putting up with any of these buzzkills, you have a clear indication of what you need to address to improve your situation. Question, challenge, and dismantle any belief that struggle is required. It's not.

A master of any craft makes his performance look easy. He has merged his acquired skill with a sense of joy and flow. You are here to master your life, not by fighting your way through distasteful situations like a football quarterback bucking a hulking defensive line, but by discovering what wants to happen, and moving with the tide of destiny. Grace implies that destiny is always working on your behalf. When you partner with Grace, it will take you to places that struggle cannot.

For many years you may have pondered, "How hard can life possibly get?" Now I give you a new question: "How easy can life get?" How much struggle can you leave behind, and how much joy can you embrace? If you are willing to question difficulty as necessity, you may be quite pleasantly surprised to find what lies on the other side of pain.

> Therefore I tell you, do not be anxious about your life, what you will eat or what you will drink, nor about your body, what you will put on . . . Look at the birds of the air: they neither sow nor reap nor gather into barns, and yet your heavenly Father feeds them. Are you not of more value than they? And which of you by being anxious can add a single hour to his span of life? . . . Consider the lilies of the field, how they grow: they neither toil nor spin, yet I tell you, even Solomon in all his glory was not arrayed like one of these.[2]

CHAPTER 12

Settle for More

A RECENT GALLUP *State of the American Workplace* poll showed that seventy percent of Americans either hate their jobs or feel disengaged at their workplace.[1] That's serious. When my book *Why Your Life Sucks and What You can do About it* was released, the publisher commissioned Gallup to ask people why their life sucks. The most prevalent response—from about thirty percent of respondents—was: "*My life sucks because of my boss.*" That's a terrible statement about the relationships that make or break business success, and establish the greater portion of our waking hours. Studies show that the day of the week and time of the day that most people die is: Monday morning at 9 AM. A lot of people would rather drop dead than go to work.

Why do so many people go to jobs they hate, and stay for many excruciating years? Why do so many workers curse their boss or company, feeling powerless to speak out or escape? Why would many people rather get sick—or die—than go to work? What makes a job feel like work?

Typical answers go something like this: *"I need the money. I have house and car payments. I have a family to support. I have training and experience in this profession, and although I am bored and tired of it, it's all I know. I don't want to have to start over. I'm afraid that if I left my secure job to pursue my passion, I will flounder and not be supported. Only eight more years until I get my retirement benefits."*

Got it. But to get to the core of why so many people stay in jobs they despise, and how to break free, we must look deeper.

We drag ourselves to distasteful jobs because we believe we have no other choice. We accept the mass agreement that work is a bummer and we must force ourselves to go every day, like it or not. We do not believe we are worth better, or that what we truly want is available. We do not see role models of people thriving and enjoying their livelihood. We have succumbed to the belief that a job is supposed to be irritating, debilitating, boring, repetitive, and life-sucking. You can tell what you believe by what you are getting. If you are getting a demeaning work life, you must believe you cannot have better.

But you *can*.

Grace never calls you to suffer—*including* your job. Grace recognizes there is a vocation you could be engaged in that wouldn't feel like work at all. It would feel like play, creativity, connection, discovery, expansion, celebration, and service. If you don't believe this is possible, you can see how far you have drifted from the vision of a rewarding livelihood.

The purpose of this book and especially this chapter is to restore that vision so you can wake up in the morning and look forward to what you will be doing this day, knowing the universe is supporting you to share your unique gifts and talents, while you contribute to the well-being of everyone you touch. If that idea stirs you, you have achieved the inception of a major course correction.

Questions worth Answering

The first step to shift to a Grace-guided career is to tell the truth about where you now stand on the continuum of career fulfillment. Answering the questions below will help you assess your current position:

1. On a scale of 1-10, how much do you enjoy your current work?

2. What elements of your work bring you reward?

3. What elements do you resist or detest?

4. Do you feel energized at the end of your work day, or do you feel beat?

5. What would it take to make going to work more attractive and rewarding?

6. How much do you enjoy your relationships with your colleagues and your clients?

7. Do you get into fights with people at your job, or feel bullied by your boss or co-workers?

8. Do you get sick or look for excuses to avoid being at your workplace?

9. Do you feel financially well compensated for your work?

10. Do you feel that you are making a meaningful contribution to the lives of others through your work?

11. Do you fantasize about another job?

12. Complete this sentence, once or many times with different answers:

Regarding my work, the truth is:

____.

13. Do you need another job to increase your sense of joy at work, or can you change, shift, transform, or upgrade elements of your current job to find more reward there?

14. If there is another job you would rather do, what step can you take to explore, acquire, or create such a position?

15. Have you shared your work-related issues, pains, joys, and visions with a trusted friend or counselor, with the intention to progress in reward in your livelihood?

16. Have you prayed about your job and asked Higher Power to help you find more personal and/or financial reward?

Your honest answers to these questions can serve as a springboard to a more constructive, creative, and rewarding livelihood. I suggest you discuss any or all of your answers with your spouse, friend, coach, or counselor, to shine more light on what it would take for you to work under Grace rather than servitude.

Grow Your Frying Pan

A fellow was a walking across a bridge when he saw a man fishing in the river below. The observer noticed that the fisherman caught a small fish and tossed it into a pail. Then he caught a large fish and cast it back into the river. He kept repeating this process, keeping the small fish and throwing the larger ones back.

Curious, the onlooker made his way down to the fisherman and asked him, "Why do you keep the little fish but throw the big ones back in the river?"

The fisherman led the visitor to his camping area and showed him a frying pan. "I have this frying pan that is about seven inches wide," he told him. "It holds only little fish. So those are the ones I keep."

Your beliefs and expectations are the frying pan in which you fry the "fish," or opportunities, that come to you during your work. If you believe you are worth just so much pay, success, or soul reward, you will attract only experiences that fit in your pan of small beliefs. If you know you are worth more, you will attract bigger and better results. The goal is to not work harder to catch more little fish. The goal is to get a bigger frying pan.

Do not limit God or the universe to your beliefs. Instead, expand your beliefs to include and embrace all that God and the universe have to offer.

If you knew that you could have a job that would deeply fulfill you emotionally and spiritually, plus pay you well, would you seek and manifest it? Such a position is available. *What you seek is seeking you.* The universe will fill your treasure house according to the size of the room you offer it. Ask for what you really want, not what you think you can get.

Now take a few moments to answer these three important questions:

What do you want?

What do you *really* want?

What do you *really, really* want?

Your answer to the third question is the most significant one. There are external things you want, and deeper inner experiences you really, really want. You may want a particular partner, house, or job, but what you *really* want is the experience of a loving connection, a sense of secure refuge, and an avenue through which you can express your unique talents and visions. When you are honest about what would satisfy *your soul*, not just your surface desires, your soul will commandeer the Law of Attraction to bring you what your heart desires. The mechanics of this process are beyond the ken of the intellect, but they are quite real and extraordinarily effective.

Your "Get Out of Jail Free" Card

One of the most popular expressions in the workplace is T.G.I.F.—"Thank God it's Friday." A large restaurant chain has even adopted this name. Most people thank God it's Friday because they do not want to be at their job, and the end of the workweek is tantamount to getting out of prison. The fact that so many people regard work as torture indicates the depth of despair to which our work life has sunk, and the call for healing it represents.

There are two ways to be liberated from work prison: (1) Leave the position that feels like prison; (2) Transform the elements that make your work feel like prison. Prison lives more *inside* of you than you live in it. If you can escape from your internal prison, you can escape from your external prison. Ultimately, everything external is a projection of the internal.

There is no profession so bereft of the potential to bless that you cannot tap into Grace and make it work on your behalf and that of your customers. On a cold winter night some friends and I were exiting the parking lot of Chicago's O'Hare Airport. As our car waited in line to go through the toll booth, I wondered what was taking so long. When we finally reached the toll booth, we found a handsome Italian man with thick white hair and sparkling eyes. As he collected our fee and handed us our change, he broke into a rousing performance of several verses from the opera *La Traviata*—masterfully sung. The women in the car swooned, we all applauded, the toll collector bowed, and we exited the parking lot with a smile. Suddenly the cold, dark night became warmer and lighter.

I later read a survey in which people were asked, "What do you think is the most boring job in the world?" The most common answer was "toll collector." If that man could turn a bleak, exhaust-fume-filled toll lane into an opera hall and transform weary travelers into an applauding audience, you and I can certainly bring more aliveness to what we do and those we touch. My mentor taught, *"Take what you have and make what you want"* —an affirmation we would all do well to apply.

A sage advised, "Choose a job you love and you will never work again." Another said, "Don't choose a job with lots of vacation time. Choose one that doesn't need escaping from." No one wants to go to a job he or she hates, and no one should. The area of your greatest pain, be it work, relationships, or health, is also the area of your greatest potential transformation.

I challenge you to never work again by either leaving a job that is shredding your soul and choosing one that enlivens you instead, or by transforming your current job so it ceases to be a burden and becomes an inspiration. Let Grace, rather than fear, obligation, history, or pressure be your cherished employer. Grace runs far deeper and broader than any company or boss, and no tyrant of an organization or supervisor can surpass the power of Grace to deliver success.

Your days were not meant to be a drudgery. They were made to inspire, uplift, and empower you and everyone you touch. A heartfelt career will leave you feeling energized, more like play than work. Such a vision of livelihood is radical, but so is every idea that has changed the world. There are people who are eager to go to their workplace each day, and you can be one of them. When you place your livelihood in the hands of Grace, it will position you precisely where you belong in the grand design of creation.

CHAPTER 13

Proof of Life after Debt

I ATTENDED A LECTURE by a fellow who claimed to communicate with a group of advanced spiritual beings. While I cannot attest to the veracity of his claim, one statement he made got my attention: "When I told them about our economic system, they were astounded. They said, 'We cannot understand why you believe you have to earn your sustenance and pay for things you want and need.'"

If you are accustomed to having to pay for everything you want and need, such a statement may seem nonsensical. The concept of inherent deservingness flies in the face of nearly everything you and I have been taught about how we acquire the stuff of life. *You must work hard (at a job you detest) to earn money. Sweat buys you the right to thrive. Nothing comes easily. No pain, no gain. Everybody owes.*

But do you really have to pay to survive? Are you required to earn your way through life? Is a sense of indebtedness a requisite for existence? Is humanity capable of transcending the law of the jungle? And if humanity is not ready to make this shift, are you? Most likely you have never thought about these questions because we just assume that owing, often beyond one's means, is just the way it is. But "the way it is" is not the way it was intended to be, or has to be, or will be.

Money as Symptom, not Cause

One of our sorest financial arenas is the amount of debt we have accrued as individuals, families, companies, and nations. In my book *Enough Already*[1] I cite staggering statistics about the amount of money people and nations owe, and the horrendous sense of financial obligation under which we labor.

Yet all of our financial indebtedness is but symptomatic of an underlying haunting sense of chronic owingness. We have fallen prey to a *debt mentality*. Your experience of debt runs far deeper than the sum of your bills. Your experience of debt stems from *how you think about* your bills, and more fundamentally *how you think about yourself*. The problem is not that you owe money. The problem is that you identify yourself as a debtor. A debtor is someone who is incomplete or insecure until his debts are cleared. There exists a gap between where you stand and sufficiency. The debtor lives in a state of lack; the condition of owingness must be offset before she can be at peace. This malaise is compounded by the Sword of Damocles that creditors hold over the debtor's head. If he does not pay, the creditor will take away his house, car, furniture, and/or money, garnish his wages, or ruin his credit score, and he may not be able to borrow again for a long time. In olden days debtors were thrown in prison. When you owe, creditors have power over your life. To owe is tantamount to giving your soul away. Many people who owe end up doing unethical or illegal acts to keep up with their payments or clear their debts; some lie, cheat, steal, or even kill. Others work at jobs they hate, make deals with people they detest, or prostitute their time and talents. Others continuously juggle credit cards, borrowing from Peter to pay Paul, walking a monthly tightrope to maintain a rickety semblance of solvency. In 1601 Shakespeare advised, "Neither a borrower nor a lender be."[2] Did he have any idea how substantially his counsel would be proven more than four centuries after he uttered it?

I am not suggesting that you should not borrow or lend. Many people acquire cars and homes, get an education, and launch businesses by taking out loans. Handled wisely, borrowing and lending can make people winners. Yet many people become losers when they sink to believe that they owe at a soul level rather than just a financial level. When debt becomes the theme of your existence, your life has become unmanageable.

Grace would have you see yourself and your life from an entirely different perspective. Grace calls you to recognize that you are whole, empowered, capable, and solvent right where you stand. Money is not a factor in the kingdom of heaven, which abides within you at this moment. The currency of heaven is love, in which you are already extremely wealthy. Where fear and ego see voids you must fill before you can become enough, Grace sees that you already stand on the ground of plenty.

Abiding in Sufficiency

Grace seeks not to fix, but to affirm. One afternoon some friends came to our house for lunch. Our guest Donna told the others that she had just come from seeing a healer who had told her that her chakras were out of balance and her body was filled with parasites. This report stimulated the group to barrage Donna with advice about how to regain her health. Donna was also dealing with a weight issue, which elicited plenty of recommendations from the gathering, based on their own weight-related frustrations.

As I listened, I cringed at the general tone of the conversation. Everyone meant well, but the theme of the talk was, "There's a lot wrong with you, and we are going to tell you how to fix it."

When Donna stepped away from the group, I invited her aside for a moment. I took her hands, looked her in the eyes, and told her, "I enjoy and respect you just the way you are. I know there are things you are working on, but right now I find you perfect and I appreciate all you are and all you do for me and others."

Tears welled up in Donna's eyes as she felt and began to let loose the pain of feeling that there were so many things wrong with her, and she could not be whole or happy until she fixed them. I sat with her and let her pour out her heart. After a while she felt better.

I was not suggesting to Donna that she overlook any conditions that were causing her pain, or that she should not make an effort to improve her health and feel better. I was simply affirming Donna's beauty, wholeness, and worth even as she walked her healing journey.

While the world judges you as imperfect until you repair what is broken, Grace does not wait for some external change to make you whole. Wholeness already abides within you. You have not borrowed anything from the universe that you need to pay back before you can start enjoying yourself. Joy costs nothing and demands nothing. Completeness is your birthright and the unshakeable condition of your existence.

How to Get Out of Debt

Certain religious beliefs and notions of karma damage people more than the economy does. Some religions teach that you are defective simply by being born, and life is an uphill battle to prove your worth and escape eternal damnation. Such primal owingness runs far deeper than any credit card bill you will ever receive. Karmic belief systems suggest that you owe from a previous life or past experiences in this life, and you must strive for many lifetimes to offset your cosmic debit. Glamour magazines and movies infer that you are less-than if you are not shaped like movie stars or display the perfect skin of photoshopped cover models. The implication of insufficiency comes at us from all angles. It is a rare family member, friend, clergyman, or teacher who tells us, "You are perfect just the way you are. There is nothing you need to fix or change, and you don't owe anything."

It *appears* that we feel indebted because we owe a lot of money. To the contrary, we owe a lot of money because *we feel indebted.* You were taught that you owe long before you got your first credit card. Your identity as a debtor was instilled many years before you received your first threatening notice that payment is overdue. If we are to get out of financial debt, we must *first get out of psychological or emotional debt.* Here's how:

1. Set your intention to dissolve from your mind any and all thoughts that "I owe" or "I must pay, lose, or sacrifice before I can be solvent and at peace."

The recognition of your inherent solvency is the ground upon which you accomplish transformation. All healing, including financial healing, is an inside job. You can jump through all kinds of hoops to fix outer situations, but before you can resolve such issues permanently you must address your attitude, identity, beliefs, and self-image. Know yourself to be a spiritual being whose true identity has nothing to do with money or what is written on papers about money. Some people owe money but they do not feel like a debtor because they know that who they are runs far deeper than their bank balance. Restore your financial well-being by restoring your identity as a wealthy soul. Remind yourself often, as *A Course in Miracles* underscores, "I am as God created me."[3]

2. Engage in a regular practice to affirm your solvency.

Each day meditate, pray, journal, speak or write affirmations, or do any exercise you choose to establish your sense of spiritual and financial sovereignty. Your mind has been trained to focus on lack; now you must re-train it to focus on abundance. Affirm, for example:

I am whole, complete, loveable, powerful, solvent, and wealthy just as I am.
I have infinite resources to do all I need to do when I need to do it.
I live under the Law of Grace.
Abundance is my natural state.
God doesn't owe and neither do I.

These statements represent your reality far more than the lack thoughts you have been telling yourself. The more you know, the less you need.

3. Identify and celebrate the aspects of your life in which you already feel whole and abundant.

Even if you owe money, there are many areas in your

life in which you are wealthy. Perhaps you feel rich in the love of your family, friends, or a pet. Or you bask in the splendor of nature. Or you play music, sing, dance, paint, or write. Notice that when you are engaged in creativity, you have no sense of debt. In any given moment of experience you cannot simultaneously create and owe. When you are creating, you are tapped into an infinite wellspring of energy, power, and aliveness. You are thriving in the image and likeness of God, privy to total fulfillment.

Neither can you feel poor when you are extending love. In the consciousness of love there is no lack. The experience of love and the experience of loss cannot coexist. To choose one is to deny the other.

4. Cease giving energy to thoughts and words of lack.

Engage in a "negation fast" in which you do not speak any words that affirm lack. Catch and redirect any thoughts engulfed in the quicksand of emptiness. Should you start to complain about a big bill or talk about the money you owe, stop—even in mid-sentence—and instead speak words of appreciation, supply, and ability.

5. Pay off your smallest debt.

Make a list of your various monetary debts and pay the smallest one off first. The feeling, "I erased that debt," will open the door in consciousness for you to feel solvent and lead you to the experience of paying down your other debts, beginning with feeling lighter and freer about your sense of debt.

6. Bless your creditors.

The more you complain about what you owe and the

people or companies to whom you owe, the more you will owe. Whatever you focus on, you get more of. When you resent the people you owe, you will find more to resent. When you bless the avenues through which providence comes to you, you will find more blessings.

I used to complain about my credit card bills. Each month when I entered the vendor and payment data into my computer, I resented the charges. I always felt worse after doing that. Then one month I decided to play the game of thanking each vendor. These companies weren't charging me for nothing; they had all provided me with valuable goods or services. I blessed each vendor as I typed their information. "Thank you, mortgage company, for helping me live in a house I so enjoy." "Thank you, grocery store, for providing me with healthy food." "Thank you, airline, for flying me quickly and safely across the ocean." By the time I was done, I felt grateful and fulfilled, and I experienced no sense of loss or lack—only supply, appreciation, and celebration. *A Course in Miracles* reminds us, ". . . each decision that you make is one between a grievance and a miracle,"[4] and "...love cannot be far behind a grateful heart and thankful mind."[5]

7. Don't take out any more loans or credit cards.

Master what is in front of you before taking on more. Don't borrow any more money or run up your credit card balance any more than you absolutely need to. (Some people initiate their journey to solvency by cutting up their credit cards.) Take charge of your life and accept responsibility to handle the debts you have already accrued. From that platform you will gain a sense of power and soundness that will set a new standard for your financial interactions.

8. Release others from debt.

The more you believe others owe you, the more oppressive your own debts will feel. I am not referring simply to financial debt, but more specifically to social or emotional debt. When you resent others for not living up to your expectations, or you grind on an insult or injustice you believe someone has inflicted upon you, in your mind you are setting up karmic debt on their part. You will not escape the debts you believe others owe you because you are living in a debt mentality and you will live under the onus of the judgments you project onto them. The more you can forgive, forget, and free others, the freer you will become to rise beyond any debts you believe the universe holds against you.

When you try to squeeze money out of people who owe you, because creditors are trying to squeeze money out of you, you perpetuate the vicious cycle. Request payment where you need to, but don't do it out of a sense of pressure, fear, or lack. Don't make your supply dependent on a particular person satisfying his or her debt to you. Your supply can come through any one of a thousand channels, and when you relax, it will.

The experience of debt is an anomaly in all of creation, a sad and debilitating story fabricated by people in a mindset of lack. Of all living things, only human beings suffer from the malaise of oppressive obligation. We are extremely clever at designing story lines that hurt us and then living in them as if they are true. The good news is that if we created the concept of debt by erroneous thinking, we can correct and heal it with right thinking.

The ultimate resolution for debt is to live in a state of Grace. In that domain, everywhere you turn, there is enough. "My cup runneth over. Surely goodness and mercy shall follow me all the days of my life."[6] Even if you are making house, car, business, college, or credit card payments, no one has a lien on your soul. Money is simply a game that people play, one you win by realizing that you are greater than any financial transaction. There is no debt in the mind of God, and there need be none in yours. Throw off the shackles of owingness by realizing that you do not, need not, and could not owe. Then, once and for all, you will attain the state of spiritual solvency that is your birthright, with all the benefits and manifestations befitting the progeny of divinity.

CHAPTER 14

When a Minus becomes a Plus

JUST BEFORE CHRISTMAS, Rob Anderson went into a convenience store to purchase three $1 Powerball lottery tickets as stocking stuffers. The clerk misunderstood Anderson's request and erroneously printed one $3 ticket. When Anderson called the mistake to the clerk's attention, he offered to nullify the ticket. Anderson decided to just go with the flow, he accepted the ticket, and purchased the three stocking stuffers in addition. Rob went home and tossed the mistaken ticket on his nightstand.

The day after Christmas the winning numbers were announced, and Anderson figured he would check the mistaken ticket just in case. It was then he realized the mistake was the happiest of accidents. He had just won nearly $129 million, the largest Powerball jackpot ever paid in the Kentucky lottery.

Sometimes what seems to be going wrong is really going right. From a human perspective it may appear that things are working against you, when they are really working for you. That's why it's important to be vigilant for the positive results apparent errors might lead to. A mistake is not a mistake if it leads to something better. Sometimes what you have labeled your biggest mistakes turn out to be your greatest blessings. Sportscaster Al Bernstein said, "Success is often the result of taking a misstep in the right direction."

Check for Fish

I once hired a woman to serve as administrator for my Life Mastery Training. Her job was to register participants and give them the information they needed to prepare for the program. A few weeks before the program I discovered that the administrator had done a very poor job of keeping records and orienting the clients. The situation was a mess; people were missing materials and they needed support. So I decided to personally phone each of the participants to see how they were doing, answer their questions, and give them encouragement toward the event.

The participants were surprised and happy to hear from me. I got logistics back on track, helped them prepare, and I enjoyed getting to know them. The experience was so rewarding for me and them that I decided to personally phone participants as a regular practice in preparation for future retreats. Since then, many participants have remarked that our conversation was one of the most rewarding elements of the program.

In retrospect I see that the registrar's mess-up turned out to be a huge asset toward my future work. The "clunk" of her taking poor care of the participants led to the real "click" of taking better care of the participants, which delivered a more fulfilling experience for me and my clients for many years to follow, as well as supporting my business. "If you fall in a mud puddle, check your pockets for fish."

What You Thought was Wrong with You may be What's Right with You

You have been taught that you are defective and lacking and you must fix yourself to become acceptable. *Nothing could be further from the truth.* You are perfect as God created you, and there is nothing you need to do to become worthy. You simply need to recognize your unique talents, trust them, and express them.

A little boy grew up in a small, poor Mexican town, in a house without running water. He was shy and unpopular, and other kids made fun of him because he spent so much time with dogs; they mocked him as "El Perrero," or "Dog Boy." At age 21 he crossed the border into the United States as an illegal immigrant, paid for by his father's $100 investment in his son's better future. Speaking no English, homeless, and penniless, El Perrero walked the streets panhandling, and hung out in a park in San Diego. There he befriended people walking their dogs and helped them improve their pets' behavior. Eventually he got a job in a dog grooming shop, where he tamed an aggressive Cocker Spaniel. The owners liked him and gave him a key to the store so he could get off the streets and have a place to sleep and shower.

El Perrero moved to Los Angeles, where he worked hard in a car wash. The owner gave him a van to start a mobile dog training business. He met actress Jada Pinkett (who later became actor Will Smith's wife) and helped her with her dog. Pinkett was so impressed with his skills that she introduced him to her Hollywood friends and paid for him to get a tutor to improve his English and become a legal citizen. In 2004 the National Geographic Channel gave him his own television show, which became a hit and fueled his worldwide reputation as "The Dog Whisperer." Cesar Milan's show, broadcast in 80 countries, has spawned five bestselling books, a line of pet products, several dog sanctuaries, generous charity donations, and a gloriously successful life for the boy once criticized for his unique passion.

If you are a misfit in one place, you will be a great fit in another. You just need to find your "just right tribe." I coach many people, for example, who have worked in the corporate world for a long time and wish to leave and create a more personally meaningful career. Some feel guilty because they have a family to provide for and they believe they should be hustling up the corporate ladder. They want to create their own business or become a coach or healing practitioner, but they fear that if they took such a leap of faith they would look weird or fail. I hear similar stories from college students who are pursuing the course of study their parents prescribed for them, while another kind of adventure keeps whispering to their heart.

Consider three men who have changed the world in a huge way: Bill Gates, co-founder of Microsoft; Steven Jobs, already noted here as co-founder of Apple Computers and founder of Pixar Animation Studios; and Michael Dell, founder of Dell Computers. None of these transformational giants finished college. Gates dropped out of Harvard; Jobs quit school to study calligraphy, which led to designing scalable fonts for the computer; Michael Dell became so successful building and selling computers from his college dormitory room that he blew off the remainder of his studies and established one of the most successful companies in the world. Consider the loss the world would have experienced if these three geniuses had stayed in college because they feared to quit.

Likewise, your own adventure calls you. You may wish to quit your job and travel; date or marry someone whose race, age, culture, religion, or gender are forbidden to you; leave a relationship in which you are smiling on the outside but crying on the inside; pursue a career that others tell you will never earn you a living; develop an invention that seems impossible; buy something extravagant; make passionate love that would make the *Kama Sutra* blush; go to an ashram instead of church; write a book about what you went through to get where you are; or push the envelope in some other unique way.

The world has rarely been changed by normal people. Nearly everyone who has made the world a better place has been considered whacko. The Wright Brothers' father was a fundamentalist Christian preacher who told his sons that their efforts to invent an airplane were the work of the devil. But "the devil knows not for whom he works." What starts out as something *apparently* evil often turns out to be very good. The Internet, for example, began as a military project. Defense honchos sought to create a decentralized system by which command posts around the world could communicate in the event that one or more centers were wiped out by a nuclear attack. From that intention the Internet technology was born, which has completely revolutionized the way we communicate, do business, and live. In contrast to its military beginning, the Internet has become a forum to bring people together for healing, constructive commerce, and social change. The 2011 Egyptian revolution, which brought down a longtime tyrannical regime, was orchestrated largely through Facebook.

The elements of your life that you have judged against yourself may be exactly the ones to celebrate. The experiences you call a pain in the ass may ultimately prove to be a pain in the asset. There is nothing that Grace cannot transform to create a blessing.

The Story Line and the Glory Line

Assume that things are going in your favor, even when they don't seem to be. Do not fall prey to appearances, which are often deceptive. You are projecting all meaning onto the events of your life, for better or worse. When you project positive meaning, you pave the way for positive results. Attitude is the strongest tool at your disposal. You cannot choose what happens, but you can choose the vision you use to interpret and manage what happens. Every minus is half of a plus waiting for a stroke of vertical awareness.

As multi-dimensional beings, we function simultaneously on different levels of experience. There is the *story line* at which negative events may occur. Divorces, financial setbacks, and illness are no fun. They hurt. They are calling for healing. At the same time, there is the *glory line*, another level of experience at which you transform hurtful experiences into helpful ones. In the Pac Man video game, Pac Man was besieged by little ghosts chasing him to gobble him up. If Pac Man was not vigilant, the ghosts would overtake him and the game would be over. But if he took the upper hand, he could capture the ghosts and they would be transformed into power nuggets. Thus Pac Man would gain energy and put more points on the board than if the ghosts had not challenged him at all.

A Course in Miracles tells us, "It takes great learning to understand that all things, events, encounters and circumstances are helpful."[1] Difficult experiences, when understood, serve as useful course corrections. Bless *all* experiences, not just the easy ones. When you find worth in an experience and gratitude for it, all experiences become your allies.

No one cruises through life without challenges. It's what we *make* of the challenges that determines the quality of our life. We create with our minds more than our hands. Let us use our minds as purveyors of Grace. Then our life becomes a series of pluses that no one can uncross.

The End or the Beginning?

What seems to be an end is really a beginning. A public park near my house leads to an exquisite waterfall further up the valley. One day I noticed that officials had posted a sign where the little-known waterfall trail begins. The sign read, "End of the Trail." Hikers unfamiliar with the area turn back when they see that sign. Yet those who know the local geography bypass it. They know that what is marked as "end of the trail" is really the beginning of the best part of the trail. Buddha said, "To see what few have seen, you must go where few have gone."

Grace is the waterfall that most people do not see because they followed the sign that told them the trail ended when it was just beginning. This book—and your life—is a course in shifting your vantage point so you can discover blessings where you saw curses; healing where you perceived pain; fullness where you perceived emptiness. It is not a course in changing yourself, for who could improve upon perfection? It is a course in falling—actually *rising*—in love with yourself.

From Breakdown to Breakthrough

Some of my biggest mistakes have led to my biggest breakthroughs. Life has ingeniously opened paths to capitalize on my errors and turn them into blessings. The universe, it turns out, is a massive alchemy laboratory. The ego screws up and the spirit turns the mess into fuel for awakening. When you realize how it all comes together, the breadth and profundity of the system is staggering.

Somehow, despite current appearances and forecasts, healing has the upper hand. Nature bats last.

Dr. Kazimierz Dabrowski wrote a book called *Positive Disintegration.*[2] As a psychologist in a mental institution, he discovered that patients who had undergone a nervous breakdown often grew psychologically healthier after their breakdown. Their life before the breakdown was so dysfunctional that to try to change it piece by piece would have been impossible. So falling apart was the best thing that could have happened to them. In the aftermath they could put their life together again in a healthier way. In that sense, their apparent breakdown was really a *breakthrough.*

The Hindu god Shiva is known as the god of destruction. While this appellation may sound negative, it is really quite positive. Replace the word "destruction" with "dissolution," and you will recognize the value in unhealthy conditions falling apart. If you look back on your life, you will see that that the situations that no longer served a purpose, or were actually working against your best interest, had to be undone to make way for something new and better. If you were keen to the signals calling for change, you consciously initiated those changes. If you were not keen to the signals, the universe initiated those changes for you. Either way, the required changes came about, always leading to an upgrade. Nothing dies without something else being born. We can celebrate the destruction of that which does not serve, or no longer serves, to make way for new, healthier creation. Shiva and the god Brahma, the lord of creation, work hand in hand to advance evolution.

Thus you are always on a tack of positive evolution. The pieces of your life that look weird, wrong, bad, or useless are key elements in the greater design of your soul's progress. You don't need to worry that you will be reincarnated as a cockroach. You know too much to make a cockroach's life interesting for you to explore. Vaster terrains call to you.

Take heart. No minus will be left standing. Ultimately everything will be plussed. What seems wrong will be righted. What seems empty will be filled. What seems dead will lead to life. What seems lost will lead to gain. Erroneously printed tickets can lead to huge wins. The universe is conspiring to bless you. Let it.

CHAPTER 15

Good News for Control Freaks

ON MY BIRTHDAY one year a friend and I went to an upscale spa for massage and relaxation. After the treatments it was time to go to dinner. "Let's go to the Greek restaurant," I told her.

"Oh, I meant to tell you," she replied, "Megan and her daughter invited us to dinner at Casanova's Italian restaurant."

I tried the idea on for size. Casanova's was a significant drive from where we were, and I liked the Greek restaurant. It didn't seem to fit. "Let's call Megan and tell her we'll see her another time," I suggested.

My friend looked troubled. "Her daughter is about to go away to school and she would like to see you before she leaves."

I started to feel irked. It was my birthday and I didn't feel like traipsing around to fulfill social obligations I hadn't agreed to. An argument ensued.

After a lengthy heated discussion, my friend convinced me that it was more important to support the girl who valued her relationship with me than to go to the Greek restaurant. We could go to the Greek restaurant anytime, but this would be the one chance to give the girl a loving sendoff. Reluctantly I agreed, but as we drove to Casanova's I silently fumed.

When we arrived at Casanova's, the maître d' escorted us to a private area where my friend and daughter were waiting. But they were not alone. As we entered the alcove, thirty of my friends stood and shouted, "Surprise!" Among the group were many dear friends I had not seen for a long time.

I was simultaneously thrilled to be honored, and I felt like an ass. All the while my friend was trying to nudge me in the direction of a huge blessing, but I was busy resisting. While I believed life was trying to hurt me, it was trying to help me. Could that be the way it always is?

How to be Truly Powerful

A seminar leader asked an audience, "Do you want to know how to be really powerful? Go to a busy intersection and stand in the center while the signal lights are changing. When the light turns green for one lane, turn toward that lane and wave everyone ahead. Then face the lane where the light has turned red, and raise your arm to stop them. Keep doing this all day, and you will be very powerful indeed."

This tongue-in-cheek example indicates that we gain maximum control by recognizing what wants to happen, or what is already happening, and aligning with it. Thus we harmonize with the natural stream of life. The Chinese master Lao Tse called this stream *The Tao*. The third Chinese Patriarch of Zen, Seng-ts'an, called it *The Great*

Way. More recently George Lucas called it *The Force*. No matter what you name it, a great symphony of life is being played at all times, orchestrated from a vantage point with far broader awareness than the small self can perceive. "The winds of Grace are always blowing," said Sri Ramakrishna. "We have only to raise our sails."

How do you know when you are moving with the Tao, or opposing it? If you feel a sense of conflict, resistance, or depletion, you are heading upstream. Activities guided by Source are empowering, exciting, and energizing. They unfold organically and are characterized by fascinating synchronicities. Activities that run counter to Source are exhausting. If you feel fatigued physically, mentally, or emotionally, you can be sure you are fighting the Force rather than moving with it. At such a point your best move is to stop, take a deep breath, and ask yourself, *"What would I be doing differently if I were motivated by joy, not fear? By willingness, not resistance? By passion, not pressure?"* Your answers to these questions will reveal a path far easier and far more productive.

At every moment there is something
that wants to happen.
When you discover what that is
and move with it,
you attain the greatest mastery
with the least effort.

Every moment is an idea whose time has come. When you recognize the gift of the moment and seize it, you will, as Thoreau said, "meet with a success unexpected in common hours" Many great inventions, for example, were simultaneously created by several different inventors. Alexander Graham Bell is acknowledged as the inventor of the telephone, but Elisha Gray had created his own version of the apparatus, for which he filed his patent application on the same day as Bell, just hours later. With a slight twist of fate, you might be paying your phone bill to Gray's descendants. While the Wright brothers were conducting their airplane experiments at Kitty Hawk, a French team was also developing the aircraft, just slightly behind Orville and Wilbur. You and I were taught that Guglielmo Marconi gave us the radio, but in 1943 the U.S. Supreme Court retroactively awarded Nikola Tesla the patent for the radio. In all of these cases, the world was ripe and ready for the new invention, and one individual who tapped into the stream of thought and delivered it to the world received credit for it. But it could just as easily have been another person. These inventions were established in the ethers, so to speak, and human beings with their antennae raised plucked them.

There are encounters, events, and relationships in your life that want to happen, opportunities laid at your doorstep. If you are busy telling the universe what to do, how, and when, you may miss out on a golden opportunity. If you deny your intuition and passion because of your preconceived idea of the way things should unfold, you will stagnate. Ride the momentum like a stallion, and it will take you to amazing places.

"Many are called, but few are chosen"[1] means that many—really, *all*—are invited, but few choose to accept their calling. Grace is the calling. Acting on Grace is the choosing.

Let Cycles Empower You

Nature moves in cycles. Everything comes around. If you understand this rhythm and act in synchrony with it, every season will be your friend. Try to buck or override natural cycles, and you will be a crispy critter. I love the word "confluence." It means "flowing together." When you are aligned with the current, you are participating in an unstoppable partnership.

Nearly everyone in the world was affected by the economic crash of 2008 and the recession that followed. Lots of people were out of work. My business was adversely affected. Attendance at my programs was down, some events were cancelled, and I had a lot more time off than usual. Rather than resist the situation and try to force things to happen that weren't ready to happen, I decided to extract a blessing from the period. I focused on being home with my family, and I used the time for prayer, meditation, introspection, creative writing, and visioning. I practiced yoga and walked in nature. I used the season to journey *inward* rather than outward.

As a result, I experienced a tremendous spiritual renewal and an extremely valuable course correction in my work and life. All the energy I had previously been devoting to office work, traveling, and teaching, was redirected to my inner growth. That year turned out to be rewarding in ways I never expected when I watched the dire newscasts about the tanking economy. Eventually the economy came around, my programs were reinstated, and my business grew even more productive because of my renewal. In retrospect I am deeply grateful for that time, which turned out not as a curse, but a gift.

During the recession I coached a woman who was panicking because her psychotherapist told her that the economy would never recover. I told her that was the most ridiculous prognostication I had ever heard. "Go stand on a beach and watch the cycle of waves," I told her. "Then watch a wave go out and tell yourself that another wave will never come in." She laughed. Then I told her, "The prediction that the economy will not recover is as outlandish as believing that a single wave, isolated out of context with the vast ocean, is the last wave ever."

When things seem to be in doldrums or going wrong, ask yourself, *"What is the gift in this moment or situation? Why has life sent this experience my way for a good reason? What can I be grateful for? How can I make this experience work on my behalf?"* To everything there is a season.[2] Don't try to ski in summer or barbecue in winter. Capitalize on what is before you rather than complaining about what is absent. Everything that seems gone will come around again somehow. Ultimately there is no loss, only change and transformation.

Near my house is a famous surf break at Ho'okipa Beach, Maui. When I drive past the bay I watch surfers hanging out on their boards waiting for the next set of waves. They are having fun talking to each other, laughing, and flirting. They are making good use of the down time. When the next wave rolls in, they jump to standing on their boards and ride. Surfers understand the ocean's cycles and work with them as a benevolent force. So it is with the ocean of life. There is a time when waves come in, a time when waves go out, and a time when there are lulls. Make use of the phase occurring at the moment, and you will be perfectly perched at all times.

The Deepest Level of Control

Where Dee and I live in the country, we occasionally see rats and mice near the house. So we got a cat to keep the rodent population down. One morning I walked into the living room and found a dead rat on the rug. After an initial "*Arrrgh*," I got a shovel and scooped up the remains, complaining to myself how gross the scene was. As I headed outside, Dee commented, "I am so grateful the cat is doing her job!"

Ah, another way of looking at the situation. We hired

the cat for a reason. Why should I complain when she fulfilled her role? Two realities presented themselves as an offering for my choice: a disgusting sight or a job well done. I decided the second option felt better, and the apparent problem gave way to a sense of gratitude.

Metaphorically speaking, we all have dead rats on our living room floor and we all have cats doing their job to keep things rodent-free. The more you complain about the dead rats, the more rats you will find. What you resist, expands and persists—this is the law of consciousness. What you celebrate also expands and persists. The more you thank the cat, the more you will find to be grateful for. The facts of events are neutral. Your interpretation creates their meaning and subsequently your experience.

Negative events that we cannot control often move us to take action we would not have taken if we had remained in a complacent rut. A cheating boyfriend, smothering girlfriend, obnoxious boss, or toxic neighborhood may motivate you to choose better for yourself. If you do, the thing you could not control was a stimulant to upgrade your life. Becoming keenly aware of what is "Not It" leads you to the awareness of what is "It," and moves you in that direction. So you can thank the adverse situation for prodding you to advance. It all ends up in the good pile.

Elvis Presley said, "When things go wrong, don't go wrong with them." "Things going wrong" is more of an interpretation than a fact. Things may seem to be going wrong at the surface level, but advancing your life at a more important level.

If you must be a control freak, assume control at the level that matters: spirit, not ego; mind, not anxious manipulation; attitudinal upgrade rather than furniture rearranging. "Who would attempt to fly with the tiny wings of a sparrow when the mighty power of an eagle has been given him?"[3] Let your will merge with universal will, and your authentic power will be the envy of kings.

CHAPTER 16

The Hard Questions

IF GRACE IS GIVEN so freely and available to all of us as our natural state, why do people suffer? Why are children starving to death while nations pay trillions of dollars to fight over oil? How could God allow eleven million people to die in the Nazi holocaust? Where was God on September 11th? Why can't we find a cure for terminal diseases? Why did my friend, a good person, die at a young age, while some very bad people live to ripe old ages? Why do greedy, unethical people bully their way to riches and power while decent, honest people struggle to pay their rent and medical bills? If I truly deserve love, why can't I find or sustain a happy relationship? Why did my husband cheat on me when I have been such a devoted wife? Why doesn't my body feel better? How could life get so bad for some people that they choose to commit suicide? Will there ever be peace on the planet?

The answer to these questions lies in the fact that you

are even asking them. To question the pain of the world means that a part of you realizes that suffering is not God's intention for humanity. Starvation, disease, and war all speak of conditions unlike our divine nature. The presence of sorrow in any form *should* bother you. The only situation more troubling than painful conditions is that people are willing to put up with them; we accept tragedies and misuse of free will as facts of life rather than the anomalies to life that they are. The acceptance of suffering as the lot of humanity is a statement of the depth of sleep into which we have fallen. If we were less tolerant of misery, we would end it sooner. Caring and compassion for those who suffer, and the deep yearning for better, are signs that we are awakening from the hypnosis of separation from God and each other. To end suffering, we must refuse to accept it as our fate.

The Crucial Shift

Troubling situations are a call for a shift in perceptive. Einstein said that you cannot solve a problem from the same level of consciousness that created it. To effectively solve problems, we must rise to a higher vantage point. That point is the recognition that at our core we are spiritual beings more than we are bodies, personalities, and the social roles with which we have become identified. You are not a body that has a soul. You are a soul that has a body. When you see yourself and others as physical beings only, you step into a mass of writhing humanity struggling for survival. That is the story at but one level of observation. Behind and beyond our human limits, we remain divine beings. Something inside you is greater than what happens to you. Your true self is deeper, stronger, and more substantial than what the world looks upon.

While climbing over an old lava rock wall I ripped my calf on a sharp rock. As I looked into the deep gash I could see muscle and the other gooey stuff the body is made of. That was the first time I had a look inside my body. It was just meat. We believe, "I am inside my body." But it is not so. There is no place inside your body where you live. If you keep looking deeper and deeper past the muscle and ligament and tissue, you will not find a "me" living in a tiny little room in your bone marrow. You have become *associated* with your body, but the *real* you lives far beyond the limits prescribed by your skin. You are an infinite spirit, with an identity and reality greater than any suffering or experience the body undergoes. The real you is indestructible and eternal.

From Death to Life

I learned about life from observing death. I was sitting with my mother when she passed away. I saw her take a breath in, then breathe out, and she did not breathe in again. When I realized she had departed, I sat with her for a while, praying, meditating, and talking to her soul. Observing her lifeless form, I realized that the body I was looking at was not my mother. Physically, yes—but there was so much more to my mother and our relationship than the body I was seeing. Her physical form was not the one who loved me and cared for me. It was the vehicle that *expressed* that love, but it was not the *source* of that love. Her love transcended the body. Many times she offered to give up her personal comforts for me. That was a decision at the level of the soul. When I realized my true mother was not the body I was observing, I entered a whole new level of relationship with her that has continued and deepened over many years. Bodies get in the way of us seeing each other as the spiritual beings we truly are. Real relationships transcend the physical form. As author Richard Bach said, "True love stories never have endings."

In my seminars I sometimes ask the audience, "Who among you has experienced communication with a loved one after he or she has passed away?" Most people in the audience raise their hand. Their departed family and friends come to them in dreams or visions, whisper in their ear, or send them signs and synchronicities.

The recognition that we are spiritual beings with infinite capabilities is the best kept secret in the world. It is, of course, not a secret at all; it has been shouted from the rooftops by every great sage and seer throughout history. Yet the masses, immersed in the shallows of life and distracted by the trinkets and petty upsets of three-dimensional existence, refuse to look deeper for the jewel of truth.

The world has historically made our invisible nature and extrasensory faculties shameful, the butt of jokes, and severely punishable. Many people have been tortured and murdered for witchcraft or stepping outside the boundaries prescribed by traditional religion. Yet when we find the courage to talk about our experiences in worlds beyond the obvious, we discover vast terrains the physical senses do not capture. I used to regularly speak to high school classes about yoga, meditation, and our spiritual faculties. We inevitably got onto the subject of psychic communication and life after death. I would ask the class, "Who here has had some paranormal experience or communication with a departed loved one?" Not one student raised a hand. When the class was over, a line of students would form to talk to me. "I heard my grandmother's voice speak to me after she died," one told me. "I know who is calling me before I pick up the phone," another reported. "I can heal people by placing my hand on the injured part of their body," said another. When I asked these students why they didn't report these important experiences in the class, they all answered, "Because kids would think I was weird." From this experience I learned that most of us are closet spiritual beings. If we told the truth about our inner lives, our reality as divine souls would be accepted, honored, and celebrated in public, and we would not have to hide or be ashamed of who we are and what we know.

Time Capsule Awakening

You have no idea why anyone is doing something, or the ultimate purpose of an experience. People go through experiences, including suffering, for reasons you do not understand. It's not that you *should* not judge. You *cannot* judge. One day all will be revealed to the recipient of that experience, including understanding its place in the greater design of one's life. Until then, trust, faith, and patience are required by both experiencer and observer.

In one of my ongoing training groups, a fellow named Ted regularly told us horror stories of the dysfunctional relationship he was in. He and his girlfriend would regularly have brutal fights, followed by passionate make-up sex. Then she didn't like his moodiness, she moved out, they missed each other, and she moved back in. Then he felt smothered, moved out, and then back in. Then she was jealous and lashed out at his female friends. Then she dated her former boyfriend to make Ted jealous. Then they bought a condo together and later sold it because they were breaking up. Then they got back together again. Brief heady highs followed by long periods of pain and discord. And on and on and on and on. (I'm feeling exhausted just writing about this!)

At first our group was sympathetic to Ted's predicament. People listened attentively and supported him. After a while the group got tired of hearing the same dramas rehashed. Finally group members told him repeatedly, "This relationship is really unhealthy, Ted. You need to end it." Ted said he agreed, but the next week he came back with another version of the same story.

The group's term ended and I didn't see Ted for a year. Then one day he phoned and told me, "I just had the most amazing realization! I realized that my relationship was really dysfunctional and I had to leave. So I did. What a great insight that was!"

Duh.

I could hardly believe that Ted thought he was coming up with this idea on his own after I and the group had told him this very fact almost weekly for a year. But he had to figure it out for himself. Until then, our words fell on deaf ears. But when Ted got it, he really got it. He had to come to this understanding in his own way in his own time. Then he owned it.

People in pain have to figure it out for themselves. Such awakening may not come in the way and time you would like or expect, but come it will. We take on experiences to gain insights. When we get the message, we can leave the experience behind and move on with the wisdom we gleaned. Such gifts, though hard won, serve us for the rest of our life and beyond.

Brilliance and Insanity

Sometimes a painful experience leads to a course correction that makes us happier in the long run. Many people report that a divorce, illness, or job loss was a key turning point of their life. These individuals were dying emotionally in loveless marriages, trudging through jobs they hated, or living unhealthy lifestyles, accepting boredom, pain, or numbness as normal or required. Then they were shaken out of their complacency. The upset was painful in the moment, but it ultimately led to a more satisfying life. Sometimes what seems like the worst thing that could happen turns out to be the best thing that could happen. In this sense, hard experiences that serve awakening are a form of Grace. A moment of suffering parted the curtain to a broader stage. As a road construction sign announced, *"The inconvenience is temporary. The improvement is permanent. Thank you for your patience."*

Our journey through Earth is an adventure to bring our life into alignment with love. Any path we choose that veers from that purpose is headed over a cliff. If we start to detour from our purpose of joy, the universe offers us a course correction. If the ego is stubbornly headed toward that cliff, that correction may seem abrupt or even violent. But if we make the correction, we will save ourselves further misery and be grateful as we reclaim our soul's true path.

Paramahansa Yogananda said that the world is a huge mental institution, and each of us hangs out in a ward with people who are crazy in the same way we are. There's the *War will Bring us Peace* Ward, the *Endless Search for my Soulmate* Ward, the *Money is Everything* Ward, the *Accumulate as Much Stuff as You Can* Ward, the *Let's Keep the Divorce Argument Going* Ward, *The Government is Doing it to us Again* Ward, and the *Just one More Self-Help Seminar will Fix Me* Ward. All of these insanities seem real and worth pursuing because lots of other crazy people in the ward agree that they are worthwhile, required, or even noble. That doesn't make them healthy. Just normal.

Despite our general insanity, we all have moments of brilliant clarity, *aha!s,* and strokes of genius that lift us up and over the institution's walls. In those moments our journey makes sense and we know that we are here for a mighty purpose. Those are the moments that make artists paint, writers write, leaders lead, and parents love their children in spite of their mistakes and misadventures. It is for those moments we live and which move us to make life better for ourselves and each other.

If the hard moments propel us toward greater life, they have served us well. They are ultimately not necessary, but if we make them necessary with our insistence to dwell to illusion, they are the allies of reality. Thank God for reality. It is far better than you have been told.

The Deepest Level of Choice

While we believe that our choices exist at the superficial level of manipulating our environment, the real level at which we have choice and power is *attitude*. Happiness is ultimately not situational. It is attitudinal. We do not suffer because of circumstances. We suffer because of the way we look at circumstances and what we make of them. Ultimately the only real choice exists in consciousness.

Many people in apparently fortuitous circumstances are miserable, while others in apparently unfortunate circumstances are soaring. Some extremely wealthy people are in tremendous psychic pain, imprisoned behind golden bars, while others with little or no money are gloriously free spirits. Some celebrities amass fame and glory that millions strive for, but commit suicide, while many little-known people live long and rewarding lives. I met a man whose grandmother had just died at the age of 113. She lived in a remote little town at the far edge of Maui, she had never ridden in a car, watched a television, or gone to a doctor. Her life was filled with the love of her family and the deepest joy. Meanwhile, many people are physically healthy and capable, but depressed. Others live in wheelchairs and are lights to the world. Happiness and suffering have little to do with what the outer world sees, and everything to do with what the inner self knows.

Let us neither succumb to the belief that you must sacrifice, be sick, celibate, or poor to be happy. Some wealthy, famous, and physically vital people have kept their priorities in order and they enjoy the gifts of Spirit even amidst abundance of health and wealth. It's all about perspective. You cannot evaluate success by circumstances. The only true measure of success is joy. We always have the power to choose joy, no matter the external appearance.

Discovering Fire

Back, now, to the big questions: why people die of starvation, war, and disease; why natural disasters take innocent lives; why apparently bad things happen to good people, while so many bad people seem to thrive. To answer these questions, one would have to look into each affected person's unique soul path and purpose. We draw experiences to us from levels far deeper than conscious choice. How and when we enter and depart life, and the stories that reveal themselves between those transition points, are chosen and orchestrated by the soul. The intellect, from its limited perspective, is not equipped to fathom higher dimensional choices. It is a tool to navigate earth, not heaven. Yet occasionally the curtain of illusion parts and we glimpse the reason for apparently unreasonable events. Suddenly the map of our journey, or a piece of it, is revealed. Those moments of clarity, rare though they may be, satisfy our hunger for purpose and sustain us when we wander. They give us faith that we are not bereft, and Grace holds us in its hand in spite of apparent chaos.

Most of the misery of humanity is caused not by an uncaring God, but by people. Human beings choose to make war, thwart food from getting to hungry children, abscond with the retirement funds of their employees, poison the earth with toxic chemicals, and commit genocide. It is we who foul our own nest. Tragic as that fact may be, a bright reality sits just on its other side. If we have cast pain upon ourselves and each other, we can choose to cast kindness instead. Even while we pray to God to save us, the power to save ourselves is in our hands. If we just quit doing things that hurt each other, the earth would quickly resemble heaven. French philosopher Pierre Teilhard de Chardin nobly stated:

> Someday, after mastering the winds,
> the waves, the tides and gravity,
> we shall harness for God
> the energies of love, and then,
> for a second time in the history of the world,
> man will have discovered fire.

The Answer to Suffering

The documentary film *Ryan's Well* recounts the extraordinary journey of seven-year-old Ryan Hreljac, who learned in school that many people in Africa do not have water. One Ugandan tribe had to walk miles each day to get water for drinking, cooking, and bathing. So Ryan mounted a campaign to raise money to build a well for this tribe. Recipients of his request recognized his sincerity, they donated, and his campaign went viral. Eventually he raised enough money to build the tribe a well. After it was completed, Ryan and his family flew from Canada to Africa to meet the tribe and see the well. Ryan was met by the entire tribe lining the road, singing a chant to him thanking him for bringing them water. Since that time the Ryan's Well Foundation has continued and expanded this humanitarian work. (ryanswell.ca)

You have the same power to make life better. You may not dig an African well, but you have your own unique sphere of influence, whether it affects one, a few, or many. You don't need to struggle to figure out who to help, nor do you have to traverse oceans to deliver mercy; at this moment life is presenting opportunities right where we stand. Steve Odland, former CEO of Office Depot and current President of the Committee for Economic Development, describes "the waiter rule."[1] He posits that you can tell a great deal about a person's character by the way he or she treats a waiter. When Odland worked as a waiter in an upscale French restaurant, one night he spilled a purple sorbet on the expensive white gown of a rich and important customer. To his surprise, she didn't admonish him. Instead, she said, "It's okay. It wasn't your fault." That experience proved pivotal in Odland's life and set a theme he has carried into all of his business and personal relationships: forgiveness trumps self-importance.

Thus we arrive at the one answer that will offset all of your questions about how to end your own sorrow and that of the world. The answer to human suffering is kindness. This may sound simplistic and obvious, but sometimes the deepest truths are overlaid with illusions that obscure the answers we seek. We each have the capacity to infuse healing into the world by treating others as if they are the same as us, not different. The Dalai Lama said, "My religion is kindness," and "If you want others to be happy, practice compassion. If you want to be happy, practice compassion." English novelist George Eliot put it nobly: "What do we live for, if it is not to make life less difficult for each other?"

Scottish theologian Ian Maclaren suggested, "Be kind, for everyone you meet if fighting a hard battle." Some battles are obvious and others are internal. Everyone who walks the earth wrestles with separateness, aloneness, and conflict. When you reach across the gulf between bodies and build a bridge from soul to soul, you defeat fear and restore humanity to the unity we were born to enjoy. There is no nobler task or privilege you can fulfill as a human being.

Sorrow is an existential paradox. It exists only to help us recognize that it does not need to exist. Some religions and spiritual paths tell us that pain is simply a fact of life; adjust and put up with it until death yields you release. But our destiny must transcend our history. The only purpose of pain is for us to learn to grow beyond it. Death is not the purveyor of respite; love is. We must lift our eyes above the world revealed to us by the physical senses alone, and embrace worlds invisible to the eye, but real to the heart.

Your inner peace is your contribution to end war. Your happiness is your contribution to end sadness. Your wellness is your contribution to end disease. Guidance and action to serve others will follow naturally. The gift you came to give is already in your hands. What you seek, Grace has already bestowed. In spite of appearances, the world is beloved by God, and all who dwell here are known and precious. May we each accept Grace and live it so richly that our lives become the answers to the hard questions we have labored to solve.

CHAPTER 17

Pray with Your Feet Moving

IF GRACE IS THE GUIDING POWER behind your life, why is your life not more graceful? Why has a merciful God not rescued you from the pain you experience or the dilemmas in which you perceive yourself to be stuck? Why doesn't all of your good flow to you naturally and organically, without much effort on your part?

It would be nice if you could just lie in bed and have checks float in through your window. With enough faith, something like that could happen. Yet ultimately you would derive more reward by participating in the manifestation and mastery of your own well-being. You have a purpose in the world besides getting checks; you have a contribution to make, insights to gain through your experience, relationships to cultivate. Grace would not rob you of your purpose. You are more blessed to participate in Grace than simply be its recipient.

If you are wondering why Grace has not helped you with your finances, job, relationship, or health, here are some reasons, along with their solutions:

1. You are not doing enough.

Ask yourself, "Have I been doing all I can on my own behalf to make my goal come about?" Have you been contacting all the people who can help you? Surfing all the related websites? Taking allied courses? Making an investment toward your success? Reaching out to potential partners or clients, or accepting those who come your way? Praying, affirming, and visualizing? Is there anything you could do more than you have been doing? If there is, you have your instructions as to what's next. You cannot expect Grace to work on your behalf if you are not working on your own behalf. As Abraham Joshua Heschel advised, "Pray as if everything depends on God, but act as if everything depends on you."

2. You are doing too much.

Overdoing can be as much of an impediment as underdoing. You may believe, "the more I do, the more likely I will achieve my goal." Yet it is not the quantity of your acts that generates manifestation. It is the *quality* of your acts, and the consciousness you bring to them. If your actions are motivated by fear and worry, doing more will not accomplish more. If your acts are impelled by faith, your acts will bear sweet and abundant fruit.

At one time I was in the market for a compost bin to turn our home's organic waste into fertilizer for our garden. I spent many hours on the Internet researching composting bins and methods. You would not believe how many ways people have invented to process garbage! There are standing bins, spinning tumblers, dual batch apparatuses, toter wheelers, multi-tiered stacked boxes, a fast-heating model, and all kinds of worms, granular starters, and stimulants you can put in the bins to accelerate the composting process. As my mind reeled with countless options, it took me a long time to make a decision. Finally I decided on a simple standing bin and I ordered it. The bin itself was not expensive, but the shipping cost nearly doubled the price of the apparatus. Finally the compost bin arrived and I set it up in my back yard.

A few days later while shopping in Costco I saw the same bin on sale for a far lesser price and no shipping cost. When I considered all the research and angst I had put into (what I created to be) a terribly complicated process, I had to laugh. The whole game could have been a lot easier if I let it. Now when I am laboring over a decision to purchase something, I ask myself, "Is this another compost bin?" When I am keen enough to catch myself, I simplify the process, follow my gut instinct, and let the complications go.

Looking back, the compost bin purchase turned out to be an extraordinarily valuable lesson, so maybe it was worth the extra money. Now I don't have to attend an expensive seminar on how to let decisions be simple!

3. You are still investing your time, energy, or money in past goals or activities you no longer prefer.

If you want to make space for the new, you must let go of the old. If you are still clinging to past relationships, business ventures, practices that no longer fulfill you, or resentments, you are blocking the arrival of something better. You have just so much space on the disk of your psyche for ideas, finances, and activities. It is tempting to continue old ways of doing things because they are known and in some ways more comfortable. But if they are no longer working for you, they are not really comfortable—

just familiar.

When considering a work project, relationship, or any life path decision, ask yourself, "Where does my passion live? If I were to follow my highest calling today, regardless of what I have done historically, what would I be doing?" If you can be honest about your answer and find the courage to step in a new direction, you will open doors the old way has closed.

4. Your anxiety about reaching the goal is blocking results from appearing.

You may be on the right track for your desired achievement, but your nervousness may be clouding your vision and repelling results from showing up. In such a situation your best tactic is to just chill and trust.

A friend of mine had a crush on a guy who passed through her town once in a while. During one pass she invited him to her house for dinner. She was so nervous that she botched the date and did not make a very good impression. The *pièce de résistance* came when she was showing him to the gate and she fell in the pond!

Fear blinds and disables. Trust and confidence clear the runway and empower results. If you are anxious about connecting with a partner, making a deal, or selling or purchasing a car or home, relax and trust Higher Power to help you with the details. It's not *all* up to you. If this partner, deal, or sale is right for you, it will happen. If not, you don't want it. Don't force or posture in a way that diminishes your peace. Good things happen in a state of *poised relaxation.*

5. You do not really want the goal you say you want.

This may be a more significant factor in your process than you realize. On a deeper level than the obvious, we choose our lives and the events that come to us, as well as the events that do not come to us. When you accept 100% responsibility for what you have created, you gain 100% of the power to create what you choose next. That's how powerful you are.

All that you attract and repel is based on your perception of cost and payoff. If you believe that the payoff is equal to or greater than the cost, you will create that result. If you believe that the cost exceeds the payoff, you will keep the result at a distance. You are always getting what you are choosing—but your choices may be operating on a subconscious level. That's why it helps to tell the truth about what you really want.

A woman phoned in to my radio program and reported that since her divorce a few years earlier, she had gained a great deal of weight and now she wanted to lose it.

Remembering the principle of cost and payoff, I asked her, "Is there any way you might believe that your weight is serving you?"

The woman replied, "The end of my marriage and my divorce were so horrendous that I feel terrified to get involved in another relationship. I believe that if I were thinner, men would find me more attractive and I would have to deal with having another man in my life. I'm just not ready for that."

This was a huge *aha!* for this woman. We talked about the possibility of her simply choosing to not be in a relationship, if she was truly not ready for one, and not needing to use the weight as a buffer against potential emotional pain. She liked that idea and decided to explore that pathway.

If you are not reaching a goal you say you want, ask yourself, "What greater reward do I perceive in *not* having this? How do I believe my current situation serves me more than getting what I say I want? Why is the goal I have identified scarier to me than staying with the way it is?" You must be extremely honest in your introspection. If you are, you will unveil the *perceived* payoff. Looking squarely at the perceived payoff will likely reveal that it is not a *real* payoff, and the payoff of achieving your goal would ultimately be greater.

6. Your desired result may come through an avenue other than the one you expect.

As I have suggested, it is important to not dictate the form in which your achievement arrives. It may come through the door you designate, but often it will come through another venue or at an unexpected time. Harrison Ford wanted to be an actor, but could not get a job. So he turned to carpentry as a vocation. One day while he was on a carpentry job he received notice of an audition. He went to the audition in his carpentry clothes, including tool belt, and got the job. That role was for Han Solo of *Star Wars,* which launched a stellar career.

If you cannot do what you are most excited about, do what is next on your list that you are excited about. When you are operating in the frequency of passion and excitement, you are in the strongest position to attract your highest good. Act with full involvement but without attachment to a particular form or result. You will be amazed at how well things work out in spite of your previous plans about how your blessings should arrive.

7. Achieving the goal would not be in your best interests, and the universe is protecting you.

Be careful what you ask for, since you might get it. St. Teresa of Lisieux said, "I thank God for not answering all of my prayers." *A Course in Miracles* asks us to remember, "I do not perceive my best interests."[1] You may *think* you know what you want, but that doesn't mean that getting it will make you happy. If your desire is born of ego, fear, anxiety, neurosis, compulsion, competition, desperation, greed, obsession to prove yourself, or any other expression of small self, be grateful that it doesn't come about. It is said, "Man's rejection is God's protection."

Here we must cite a corollary to the Law of Attraction: *The Law of Repulsion.* This means that what doesn't match you will be repelled from you. If you eat a food that is poisonous or indigestible, your body will reject it. So it is with lovers, friends, jobs, and living situations that do not match you. No matter how hard you try to force a jigsaw piece into a space unlike its form, it won't fit. There is another piece that belongs in that space, and another space where the ill-fitting piece belongs. That's in your favor. Why would you want someone or something that doesn't match or belong to you?

When you say, "Not my, but Thy will," you are inviting the universe to deliver you the highest blessings. If your relationship or project is going nowhere, your best move may be to step back from your anxious efforts and say, "Okay, God, I don't claim to know what is in my best interest here. If this relationship or job is right for me and everyone involved, bring it on. If there is something better for me, I open to receive that." I assure you this prayer will be heard and you will find yourself in the optimal position with the least effort on your part.

Is your life predetermined by God, or are you called to create your own destiny? The answer is: *Both.* It's not either/or. It's *both/and.* God helps you through other people and events, and God helps you through your own actions. If you weight the equation too heavily toward one extreme or the other, you will be out of balance and not enjoy your desired results. Find the sweet spot of Grace from the outside world and Grace from within, and you are primed for the best ride.

You are an expression of God in life, a channel for your own blessings. Grace needs you as much as you need it. Help the universe help you by doing all you can on your own behalf. Then you will experience co-creation at its finest.

CHAPTER 18

Then a Miracle Happens

IN THE CLASSIC MOVIE *The African Queen,* a couple fleeing from war boards a dilapidated steamboat to make their way downriver in hopes of reaching Lake Victoria. Along the way they encounter all manner of threats and trials, from hostile German soldiers to raging rapids to blood-sucking leeches, mosquitos, and wild animals, compounded by their stubborn personality differences. Finally, as if the gods have laid a final-blow curse upon them, the river dries up and the ship runs aground in a mucky swamp, high weeds blocking views in all directions. The two are stuck and apparently doomed. Exhausted and disheartened, they lie down in each other's arms, surrender to death, and fall asleep.

As the two slumber, the camera slowly rises to a perspective high above the boat, affording a broad overview of their situation. Ironically, the ship is just around the bend from Lake Victoria, obscured by thick jungle. Then overnight something miraculous happens: rain comes.

And it comes in plenty, swelling the river, lifting the boat from the muck, and propelling the African Queen and her two passengers downstream. When the couple awakes in the morning, to their surprise and delight, they find themselves at the mouth of the river, entering the body of water they have fought so vehemently to reach.

This scene offers a striking metaphor for how Grace works: Just when you think you are finished, a blessing comes and propels you to complete your journey. You had to do your part, but then God had to do God's part.

Just Start

Many of my coaching clients tell me that they have a vision of creating a successful business, relationship, or adventure—but they do not know how to accomplish it. Since they do not know how to finish, they are afraid to even start. I tell them, "You don't have to know how to finish. You just have to know how to start." Great enterprises unfold one step at a time. Each new step is revealed as you complete the previous one. I ask such clients, "What would be the first step, even a baby step that you could take to begin this project?" Usually they are aware of even a little something they can do. I tell them, "Do that little something, and as you become more experienced and excited about the domain you are exploring, the Law of Attraction will bring more of the same your way." An object at rest tends to stay at rest, and an object in motion tends to stay in motion. Give your project an initial push, and that push will gather momentum.

When you are clear on the "what," the universe will take care of the "how." Many people use lack of skill, experience, or knowledge of a field as an excuse not to begin a desired project. Yet it is actually fear or a sense of inadequacy that is stopping them. Perfectionism is procrastination. If you believe you have to know everything about your project or do it all perfectly, you are simply delaying getting going. You learn by doing, not waiting. If everyone had to wait until they were a perfect parent to become a parent, there would be no children. You *become* a good parent by *being* a parent. Likewise, you become adept—even *great*— at what you seek to master by diving in.

It is but ego that believes you must figure it all out before you can start—or finish. Spirit, on the other hand, makes masterful use of the Grace factor. God will fill in the blanks that you cannot. Steer your boat to the mouth of the river. Then the rains will come and lift you into the lake.

Leave Space for a Miracle

A cute cartoon shows a professor writing a long physics equation on a wall-wide blackboard. Midway through the equation there is a gap in which the words are written, "Then a miracle occurs." While this formula would not hold up under the laws of traditional physics, it holds up under the Laws of God. (And it may even hold up in the more forward-thinking quadrant of quantum physics.) One of my favorite lessons from *A Course in Miracles* is, "I am under no laws but God's."[1] While we labor under a myriad of onerous human laws (based largely on fear, insecurity, and mass agreement), ultimately we are subject only to the Laws of God, which are founded on Love and Grace.

If you are struggling with a difficult question or situation, leave space for a miracle. If you are stubbornly trying to do it all yourself, Higher Power has a harder time wedging help into the cracks. Healing is freely and generously given, but it requires your acceptance. Allow God to help—better yet, *invite* God to help. Do all you can do, and when you can do no more, leave the rest in the hands of God. Your faith will be justified.

Launch and Release

In the last chapter we focused on the importance of taking action to follow up your prayers. There is yet another step after action: *Release your efforts to the universe.* If you keep acting beyond a certain point, you are in effect saying, "My prayers have not been heard, so I better keep plugging away at this," or "The success of this project depends on me alone." In such a case your prolonged efforts are not a statement of faith, but *lack* of faith. You are usurping the role of God. Genuine success is a co-creative effort between you and What is beyond you. Whether or not you realize it, you are partnered with Higher Power. After you have done all you can, let God do all God can. All spiritual ventures are shared between the human and the divine. When the two merge, greatness manifests.

It is said that "man's extremity is God's opportunity." When you feel like giving up, you are in the prime position to receive help. Not that you should surrender lazily. But when you have done all you can and you can do no more, it may be time to give up. Consider the phrase, "give up." You are giving your situation up to a Higher Power, placing it in the able hands of God, to do for you what you cannot do for yourself.

If your life is falling apart or has fallen apart, there is a better life waiting for you. If your life was working, it would still be in place. But it, or a part of it, was not working, and you doggedly kept trying to make it work. A Chinese adage suggests, "If your horse dies, get off." Many of us have tried to ride dead horses of relationships, jobs, or living situations, and we wondered why we did not get anywhere. When we give up trying to uphold a dysfunctional situation, Grace leads us to a greater good. Nothing is ever taken away without something better showing up to replace it.

In a sense, coming to the end of your rope is the best thing that can happen to you. A better, longer, stronger rope is swinging toward you. Quit trying to work your way back up the old rope. It is not tied to anything. The new rope is attached to where you want to go.

Like the voyage of the African Queen, many of us perceive our journey as a long series of battles against adverse sources. We believe we must fight off everyone and everything that attempts to thwart us, with no end in sight. Yet there is an end, and even though it may not be in sight at the moment, it is there. More precisely, it is *here*. Metaphysically speaking, the goal has *already* been reached. When you accept achievement as a foregone conclusion, you hasten its manifestation. *Proceed as if success is inevitable.*

As you write your equation for success on the blackboard of your life, leave space for a miracle to enter. The space signifies that you are inviting and allowing God's power to achieve for you what you cannot achieve for yourself. The universe is fully capable to take care of you if you let it. Trust the river to carry you to your destination. And should the river dry up momentarily, the source of the river, which flows from the heavens, will enable your final step. Be not dismayed by the weeds and jungle that momentarily obscure your view. The haven you seek is just around the bend.

CHAPTER 19

The Quality of Mercy

The quality of mercy is not strained;
It droppeth as the gentle rain from heaven
Upon the place beneath. It is twice blest;
It blesseth him that gives and him that takes.
—William Shakespeare[1]

IN MY BOOK *A Course in Miracles Made Easy* I recounted the astonishing story of Wesley Autrey, who, while waiting for a Manhattan subway train, watched a young man be overtaken by an epileptic seizure and fall off the platform into the path of an oncoming train. In a flash, Autry jumped onto the tracks, covered the man's body with his own, and pushed himself and the fellow into the gutter between the tracks. The train, unable to stop, hurtled over the two men. When it finally passed, onlookers were amazed to see both men emerge unscathed. The train had passed so close to Autrey's head that his ski hat was smudged with grease from the train's undercarriage.

Yet there is more to the story. In an NPR interview following the incident, Autrey revealed that years earlier a street thug had pointed a gun at his head and pulled the trigger. Miraculously, the gun did not go off. "I figured I still had a purpose on earth," he remarked. "Maybe helping the man who fell was why I had to stick around."

While most people are primarily concerned with our own needs, we have the capacity to rise above the instinct for self-preservation and perform acts of mercy that are nothing less than angelic—even miraculous. For one man to risk his life for another, as Autrey did, reveals the divine spark within all of us that can turn a hell of world into heaven on earth. Such a gift of mercy proves not just that we can be more, but we *are* more.

At Our Best when Things are Worst

When Captain Chesley B. Sullenberger III piloted his U.S. Airways airplane to take off from New York's LaGuardia airport on a cold January morning, he had no idea where that flight would take him. Shortly after take-off, the Airbus 320 encountered a flock of birds that were sucked into its jets, instantly disabling flight. With no landing strip in range, Sullenberger's only option was to set the plane down on the Hudson River. As the pilot executed a skilled landing on the icy waters, the crews of nearby ferry boats saw the crash and motored to the plane to rescue the passengers. Sullenberger's true bravery came forth when he made his way through the aisle of the sinking aircraft to be sure no one was left aboard. When he was certain that all of the 150 passengers and 5 crew members had exited safely, he stepped across a wing to helping hands.

Then there were the ferrymen who rushed to the passengers' aid, along with the coast guard, police, and firemen. Emergencies have a way of calling forth our higher nature. When there is trouble, something in us wants to help—something bigger than the situation or the fear it might engender.

The movie *Starman* tells of an extraterrestrial who visits Earth by cloning the body of a man who has recently died. The cosmic visitor meets the man's widow, who, although initially petrified, proceeds to help him. Starman spends the larger part of his earthly visit fleeing from authorities attempting to capture him. Smarter than his pursuers, he eventually engineers a rendezvous with a rescue starship. Moments before he departs, he confides in a human companion, *"Shall I tell you what I find beautiful about you? . . . You are at your very best when things are worst."*

In another famous movie, *Schindler's List,* based on a true story, Nazi Lieutenant Amon Goeth is bragging to business mogul Oskar Schindler about how powerful he is, able to kill masses of people with a single command. Schindler, a compassionate German who is using his wealth to help Jews escape the Holocaust, tells Goeth, "Power is when we have every justification to kill, and we don't."

Our life is a journey from the temptation of worldly power to the acceptance of divine power, characterized by the demonstration of mercy. Worldly power manipulates and controls. Spiritual power releases and redeems. The true sign of spiritual maturity is the willingness to give love rather than seek it. Abraham Joshua Heschel declared, "When I was young, I admired clever people. Now that I am old, I admire kind people."

What Really Matters

One of my heroes is the visionary inventor Nikola Tesla. Little known and extraordinarily under acknowledged, this mystic scientist is responsible for much of the technology that powers our world. Tesla gave the world alternating current (AC) electricity, wireless technology, the radio, radar, robotics, x-rays, Fluorescent lighting, and much more. If you use any appliance you plug into a wall socket; talk or text on a cell phone or send emails or surf the Internet via Wi-Fi; listen to a radio; change television channels with a remote control wand; or have ever had an x-ray; you can thank Nikola Tesla, a genius far ahead of his time.

Tesla traveled from his native Serbia to America in 1884 with a letter of introduction to celebrated inventor Thomas Edison. Edison took Tesla on as an assistant for a salary of $14 a week and offered him a bonus of $50,000 (equivalent to far more than a million dollars today) if he could improve Edison's electrical system. Tesla went ahead and did exactly that, and when he came to Edison for his bonus, Edison told him that he was just joking.

Tesla went to work as a ditch digger in New York City, meanwhile formulating in his mind electronic inventions based on visions that crashed into his brain like the lightning he strove to harness. He was discovered by George Westinghouse, who recognized Tesla's genius and potential. The two partnered to create the Westinghouse Company, in which Tesla had a contract to receive $2.50 for every kilowatt of electricity the company sold. Westinghouse developed alternating current technology and went on to electrify the world.

As years passed, Mr. Westinghouse made poor investments that practically wiped out the company. Being a man of integrity, he came to Tesla and promised him that one day he would make good on their contract. Tesla took the contract and ripped it up. He thanked Westinghouse for believing in him and helping him bring electricity to the world. For Tesla, that was enough. Had he collected on the contract, his estate today would be worth many billions of dollars. But Tesla cared more about service than money. His contribution to our world cannot be overestimated.

It Takes Just One

Caine Monroy, age 9, lived in a poor section of East Los Angeles. Having no money to buy electronic games, Caine fired up his imagination during a summer vacation and created an elaborate cardboard arcade in his father's used auto parts shop. He fashioned an array of pinball games, skee-ball, and claw capture games with only cardboard, tape, a marking crayon, and recycled materials. Then Caine printed tickets and waited for customers. But since his dad's business had few walk-ins, Caine waited for the entire summer. Finally a customer named Nirvan Mullick showed up at the shop seeking a replacement for a car door handle. Mullick was so impressed with Caine's ingenuity that he organized a flash mob to patronize the boy's enterprise. Mullick took Caine out for lunch, and when the two returned, the boy found hundreds of enthusiastic people lined up to play in his arcade. What a thrill for the boy!

That was just the beginning. Television and news services got wind of the venture and produced feature stories on Caine's endeavor. Actor Jack Black brought his family to play. Then Mullick organized an Internet crowdfunding effort to create a college fund for Caine. The goal was $25,000, and to date donations exceed $241,000. As word of Caine's project spread virally, schools and communities around the globe participated in *Cardboard Chal-*

lenge, with over 85,000 participants in 46 countries creating extraordinary machines with cardboard. Their ingenuity is astounding! (To track this adventure, visit cainesarcade.com or cardboardchallenge.com.)

It took only one man to believe in Caine to change his entire life, and infuse creativity into the lives of many thousands of others. Believing in someone is an act of mercy. Most people have been judged, criticized, invalidated, and emotionally beaten down to the point that their self-image has shriveled and their creativity vaporized. They do not perceive that anyone believes in them and they do not believe in themselves. If even one visionary friend finds the light in you and fans the flame, your life becomes a whole new story. If you find the light in one person and magnify it with your attention and support, you rise above the mire of worldly negation and infuse love in a space once bleak. The encouragement you give does not stop with the recipient. It will expand through routes far beyond your imagination.

Mercy to Self

While it is important to extend mercy to others, it is equally important to extend mercy to yourself. You deserve the kindness and forgiveness you wish for those you care about. If you release others from fear, pain, guilt, and obligation, but you do not let yourself out of those dank prisons, a gap of darkness remains in a universe of light.

Self-beating is not a part of God's plan. You may remember the character Silas in the book and film, *The DaVinci Code*.[1] Silas regularly flagellated himself with metal hooks until he bled. While many religions demand *mia culpa* in various forms, self-punishment is not the will of God and does not engender happy, healthy, productive human beings.

My friend Lou entered a monastery at a young age. There he was instructed to beat himself daily with a leather strap. All the monks were ordered to shower while wearing their undershorts to avoid sexual stimulation. Meanwhile many of them were engaging in homosexual activities behind closed doors. You cannot beat natural impulses like sexual instincts out of yourself. In the absence of healthy outlets they will find their way into expression via subterfuged passageways. Instead, channel your impulses into loving expression. True love does not require closed doors.

Lou left the monastery to become a public high school teacher. There he found that the educational system did not inculcate the students' deep creativity, so he talked his supervisor into allowing him to offer a class called *Humanities.* In this course he focused on his students' talents and aspirations. Lou would invite each student to sit in a director's chair in front of the class, where he conducted an intimate conversation with him or her. "How's it going at home for you?" he would ask. "What are your joys and passions, your fears and your pains?" "If you could do anything you wanted with your life, no limits, what would it be?" Lou set up activities in which the students engaged in lively interactions with the community. At Halloween he invited a group of senior citizens to come into the class, where the kids and seniors dressed up as each other. On Thanksgiving he took his classes to a homeless shelter to feed the hungry. He fanned the spark of passionate exploration in his students and made all of life their classroom.

The students loved this course and Lou was consistently voted favorite teacher in the school. This elective class became so popular that before long he was teaching six periods of *Humanities* each day. Then the school hired two more teachers to present the course full time, as well. Lou and I shared a house for a year, and during that time he regularly received phone calls from former students telling him that his class above all others had prepared them for life.

Lou's early experience in self-beating stimulated him to value self-honoring as he matured. He became kind to himself, which spilled over to kindness to others. His pain pushed him into compassion and service that benefitted countless souls. *A Course in Miracles* tells us, "A miracle is never lost. It may touch many people you have not even met, and produce undreamed of changes in situations of which you are not even aware."[2]

At Whose Mercy?

I received an email from a woman whose husband had fainted on the golf course and had to be taken to the emergency room. The husband was undergoing a series of tests to determine what had caused the collapse. She wrote, "We are at the mercy of the doctors."

Something about that phrase got my attention. I don't believe that anyone is at the mercy of another person. In the realm of appearances, it certainly may look that way. But appearances do not hold up under the lamp of truth. Ultimately you are only at the mercy of God. Because God is completely merciful, total mercy is always granted. Drop any idea that you are at the mercy of a person or persons. People are channels of mercy for Higher Power, and blessed are those who give it. Those who do not give it are not in alignment with their purpose or yours. Ask God for mercy, and it will come through the appropriate channel in the right way at the right time.

Behind and beyond appearances, life is offering you mercy. The world lives by rules that bind human beings into ever tighter cages, and mercy appears to be the exception. News reports occasionally highlight stories of kindness and forgiveness, but they are rare and by far overshadowed by accounts of mayhem. Yet in a world racked with punishment, mercy is the only story worth telling.

One night in Charleston, South Carolina, a white supremacist entered the Emanuel African Methodist Episcopal Church, and shot nine people to death. His intention was to start a race war. Yet the families of the victims refused to go there. They made a public statement that they forgave the killer. An act like that, magnified by media coverage, has the power to tilt the world in the direction of sanity and healing, and end the suffering under which humanity has so long labored. Many people shouted that the killer should not be forgiven. But forgiveness does not imply approval, condoning, or indifference. It implies that the forgiver refuses to perpetuate the dark and fruitless cycle of retaliation or to infuse the venom of hatred that caused tragedy.

At every moment we choose whether we will worship at the altar of fear, or love. The Autreys, Sullenbergers, Teslas, Mullicks, Schindlers, teachers like Lou, and the families of the African Methodist church are harbingers of mercy. They represent who we can be when we remember that the presence of Spirit is more powerful than the letter of the law. Ultimately only God's laws stand, and they are based entirely on the recognition of our inherent worth. The quality of mercy is not strained. It droppeth as the gentle rain from heaven.

CHAPTER 20

Happy Outcomes Assured

I DREAMED THAT MY FRIEND Michelle had just gone through a painful breakup with her boyfriend. She felt devastated because she had thought this fellow was the man of her dreams and they would be together for life. Heartbroken and discouraged, she feared to face her future.

In the dream, I was telephoning Michelle from two years forward in time. From that vantage point I knew what had happened since her breakup. During that time she had met a wonderful man, they had married, and she was very happy. The breakup was of no consequence now; in fact, it had placed her in a position to meet the fine fellow who had become her husband.

On the telephone I told Michelle, "Please listen to me. I can see your life from two years ahead of where you are now. I know what will happen because from where I am standing it has already happened. Soon you will meet a wonderful man and you will be happily married. You've got to believe me."

As I awoke from the dream, the words, "you've got to believe me" ruminated in my mind. My sense of confidence and fulfillment was paramount. It occurred to me that this is exactly what God, our angels, and our spirit guides are saying to us when we feel disappointed, frustrated, depressed, or heartbroken. They are in effect phoning us and saying, "Please listen to me. I am standing in your future, and I can tell you with perfect assurance that the thing you are worrying about now will become as nothing to you. Everything is going to turn out all right. You've got to believe me."

Not the End Yet

In the film *The Best Exotic Marigold Hotel,* a group of elders travels to India to stay in a retirement home. There they meet hotel manager Sonny, a likeable huckster who falls all over himself trying to keep his guests happy in their substandard facilities. When one of the residents comes to Sonny with a problem, he tells her, "Everything will be all right in the end. If it's not all right, then it's not yet the end."

A Course in Miracles lesson promises us, "A happy outcome to all things is sure."[1] The ego, or limited version of self, tells us that our problems are insurmountable and we will never get out of the jam(s) in which we perceive ourselves to be stuck. When you are in the middle of a problem, it may seem impossible to solve. Yet the Spiritual Eye sees a far vaster terrain. It recognizes that all of our problems will at some point be solved. "Thoughts held in mind create results of their kind." So don't dwell on the problem. Dwell on the solution. Even if you don't know what is the solution is, know that it already exists and will manifest.

Consider all the things you have worried about over

the course of your lifetime. At the moments you faced these challenges they seemed solid and perhaps unsurpassable. Yet over time they have been handled. Your current issue is no exception. Fear would have you believe that this problem is an exception to the presence of love. It is not. There are no exceptions to the presence of love.

Practicing the Presence

Brother Lawrence was a seventeenth-century Carmelite lay brother who wrote a now-classic book, *The Practice of the Presence of God.*[2] One day Brother Lawrence looked at a barren tree in winter, stripped of leaves and signs of life. He realized that in spite of current appearances, when spring arrived, vitality would return, and new leaves and flowers would burst forth on the tree. Suddenly the stark tree "flashed in upon my soul the fact of God." From that moment on, Brother Lawrence devoted his life to recognizing God wherever he stood.

Brother Lawrence's faith and joy were so radiant that he attracted many people to seek him out for guidance and solace. He worked in the monastery kitchen and used every moment to discover the divine. He is noted for saying,

> The time of business does not with me differ from the time of prayer; and in the noise and clatter of my kitchen, while several persons are at the same time calling for different things, I possess God in as great tranquility as if I were upon my knees before the Blessed Sacrament.[3]

It's easy to thank God when things are going well, and we should. Yet the most powerful time to practice the presence of well-being is when appearances indicate its lack. When you have a problem that you don't know how you are going to remedy, you have a golden opportunity to establish your consciousness in the condition of solution. To find heaven in the midst of hell is to spell the end of evil. While the mortal mind perceives a problem, our far-seeing vision embraces resolution. Either God is present or God is absent. There is no in-between. People flocked to be with Brother Lawrence because he recognized the presence where others did not. Brother Lawrence was no closer to God than you and me. His eyes were simply open to the treasure given to all of us.

Through a Glass Darkly

In his famous letter to the Corinthians, Paul observed that "we see through a glass darkly."[4] We do not see things as they are. We see our *beliefs* about what they are, *our version* of the universe. If our beliefs are colored by fear, mistrust, emptiness, or expectation of failure, we see amiss and we will generate negative results—not because that's the way things are, but because we have with the power to create experience with our thoughts. Before we can correct the situations about which we are concerned, we must correct our *vision* of them. The prerequisite for all positive change is *metanoia,* a Greek word meaning, "transformation of the mind." Paul also said, "Be renewed by the renewing of the mind."[5]

It is natural and healthy that you want any distressing situations in your life to be gone now. A part of your mind recognizes that pain is a mismatch to your soul and you seek the restoration of your deserved state of wellness. Yet appearances encroach on truth, and it *seems* that you are separated from your solution. But you are not. Your solution will come. The pain you feel or the fear you face will be lifted and you will return to peace. Nothing will be left unresolved. The universe is not done with you until everything is handled. Positive endings are already set. The ending may not take the form or timing you are trying to squeeze it into, but if you knew that the completion would be a happy one, would you care about the form?

In the film *Shakespeare in Love*, theatrical entrepreneur Philip Marlowe keeps getting into trouble. Yet he always says, "Everything will work out," and somehow it does. When he is asked how this process works, he answers, "It's a mystery!" Miracles pose a mystery to the intellect, but they are quite natural to the spirit. *A Course in Miracles* tells us, "You are entitled to miracles."[6] Only the deluded ego tells us that we are punishable, and suffering is required. Happy outcomes are your birthright. Now is the time to claim them.

The same voice of solace that spoke to Philip Marlowe also lives in your mind. When things seem dark you must call that voice forth to center stage. God dwells at the heart of your being, rather than the evil you have been taught lives there. The idea that you are defective and deserving of pain is a delusion of insane magnitude, the most ludicrous scam ever perpetrated. You deserve only happy outcomes, and you shall have them. If it's not all right, it's not the end yet. You've got to believe me.

CHAPTER 21

Everyone Goes to Heaven

THE SHORT FILM *Admissions* (admissionsfilm.com) offers a striking model of healing. Three people who have just died find themselves in an afterlife reception area, awaiting judgment. On the far wall we see two doors, one marked "Heaven" and the other "Hell." An admissions officer talks to the newly-arrived group about their earthly lives. Two of the people are Israeli Jews. The other is an Arab terrorist. All of them have huge blocks to forgiveness, which they must confront within the short time before judgment is passed. Finally the door to heaven opens for the Israelis, and they enter. Meanwhile the Arab awaits his judgment, fearing he will not be admitted. To his surprise, the door to heaven opens for him as well. As he is about to enter, he points to the door marked "Hell" and asks the admissions officer, "Does anyone go through that door?" The officer shakes his head, offers a small smile, and explains, "That's just a prop."

Hell is an invention of the fearful mind, not the creation of God and certainly not God's intention for His beloved progeny. It is the experience that results when we deny the presence of love in and around us. Heaven is freedom from the limits imposed by the judgmental mind and physical body. Without contracting our awareness to the stifling intellect and narrow physical senses, we see afar. Hell is fear and heaven is love. This simple truth dissolves all the complicated illusions you have been taught about life, death, here, and hereafter. There is no hereafter. There is only here. There is no afterlife. There is only life.

If you believe that other people must go to hell, so must you, for we do not escape the judgments we lay over others. Yet not to worry. You will not be consigned to the fiery pit for eternity. But you will suffer while you cling to judgment. Not because God is punishing you. Because judgment constricts your mind and heart to such a miniscule world that you miss the experience of love you were born to enjoy. We punish but ourselves with the judgments we hold. And we release ourselves with the forgiveness we offer. It is not God's forgiveness you require. It is your own. You must forgive before you can recognize that you are forgiven. We are all forgiven by God, now and after we depart from this dimension. Your soul is not subject to human frailty, whim, or illusion. What God created is perfect, untouchable by what we call sin. Your true nature is eternal innocence. All else is the mistake of a mind drunk with delusion.

After the Makeup is Removed

Tales of eternal hell were concocted by fearful people trying to control your behavior. No one who truly loves you would want to scare you into doing what they prefer. People who feel guilty attempt to manipulate others through guilt. People who feel powerless attempt to manipulate through control. Fearful people try to scare you. Hell is simply the projection of a fearful mind. Heaven is the extension of an innocent mind. We all have the capacity to fabricate heaven or hell, and then live in the results of our creation.

The world you see is a motion picture of your thoughts projected onto people and events. Everyone you meet is a character in the movie you have produced. Actors are not the characters they portray. Some actors take on mean and nasty roles, performances that make you cringe and boo. But they are just good actors. The fact that they got you so riled means they are excellent actors. A less talented actor would make the story quite boring and no one would watch it.

We get fooled when we believe in the role more than the actor. My friend Lena was a well-known actress in a popular television soap opera. She played a nasty conniving woman who continuously manipulated for self-serving purposes. When Lena left the television studio after her performances, fans of the show were waiting for her at the stage door. "You bitch!" they yelled at her. "How could you do that to Ross? He is such a nice guy. You should be ashamed of yourself!" Then they would give her stink eye and flip her the bird.

Lena was actually a kind, gentle, lovely woman. She was just a good actress. Her fans believed she was her role, so they missed out on the quality person she really was. Life outside the television studio is not much different. It's all a big soap opera.

Segue into Light

In Japan I visited Hiroshima, where the first atomic bomb was dropped. At the center of the city, a short distance from where the bomb fell, there is now a serene, tastefully landscaped park to commemorate the incident and inspire visitors toward peace, so that such a horrendous event might never occur again.

In the Peace Park stands a museum dedicated to the memory of the 80,000 people who lost their lives as a result of the bombing. On a museum wall I beheld an electronic display of photographs and names of the victims of the bombing. I found it sobering to see that these were real people, mothers and children, fathers and grandparents, teachers and waitresses and taxi drivers and students—not just a faceless mass. My heart opened with compassion for the suffering these people, their families, and ultimately the entire world has undergone as a result of this heinous act of war.

Because the walls of the museum do not have space to display the photos of all 80,000 people, the curators created a brilliant way to show all the images. A panel containing a group of about 100 photos appears on a large LCD screen, remains in view for a few moments, and then fades to be replaced by the next 100 photos. The *way* the photos segue got my attention. The pictures don't just blank out. They gradually fade into light. When the images have completely merged into the light, the next group slowly emerges from the light into form. This process goes on until all the photos have been displayed.

I considered the symbolism that all the people who were killed in the bombing dissolved into light. The men and the women, the young and the old, the beautiful and the ugly, the wealthy and the poor, the religious and the atheists, the so-called righteous and the so-called sinners. When it was time for each of them to exit, they all merged into the same vast pool. I took comfort in knowing that everyone who was killed in that dark moment in the physical world went home to the light. The dark moment was fleeting; the light is eternal.

How to Conquer Evil

If everyone goes to heaven, and we are all equally loveable, valuable, innocent, and forgiven in the eyes of God, does this mean that we are to overlook or condone acts of evil? Does everyone have *carte blanche* to steal and rape and kill? Are we to let people drive drunk? Look the other way while priests molest children? Release prisoners to roam the streets and hurt more people? Stand aside as nations bully one another and wage wars of greed?

Certainly not. There are acts that yield happiness and well-being, and others that deliver pain and sorrow. We must discern between the two and foster actions that alleviate suffering rather than perpetuate it. We must affirm what helps and stop what hurts. So live your life with the noblest ethics and morality you can; teach your children right from wrong; do not tolerate misconduct; reward kindness; stop abuse and end violence. "First do no harm." All the teachings of the great religions and philosophers point toward this end.

Meanwhile remember the bigger picture. We are all created in the image and likeness of God. Even Hitler, at the core of his being, was a spiritual soul. That soul was covered with unbelievable mire and illusions, to the point that he perpetrated unthinkable atrocities on the earth plane. But behind the horrid role he played, the core of him was still beloved of God. Hitler was severely caught in illusion and delusion. If you fear, hate, or punish Hitler or his like, so are you caught. The way to vanquish tyrants is to rise above the fear, pain, and separation that moved them to do what they did. No one who recognizes the spark of divinity within himself would wage war, commit genocide, or kill schoolchildren. The cure for aggression is not to add more pain to the world. It is reconnection to Source. The more you stay connected to Higher Power, regardless of whether or not those are around you keep or lose their connection, the closer you bring the world to healing. Your most vital contribution to the planet is your own inner peace. To stay sane in the midst of insanity gives you leverage to heal insanity. Simply: Don't go there.

All in this Together

There is a reason we all have an investment in the Hitlers, Husseins, and Mansons of the world going to heaven. Your salvation depends on theirs. Unless Hitler gets to eventually find his way to heaven, neither do you. What you allow for others, you allow for yourself. What you deny others, you deny yourself. You cannot judge without feeling judged and you cannot forgive without feeling forgiven. Forgiveness is a gift you give to others, but more fundamentally it is a gift you give *yourself.*

We enter the gates of heaven all together or not at all. The key is to recognize the splendor and wholeness within every soul, including yourself, rather than dote on the dark appearances the world finds so fascinating. Whatever you are fascinated with, you get more of. Even while humans are fascinated with our sins and those of others, God is fascinated with our holiness. Grace does not know sin. The door to heaven is open now, and always will be. The other door is just a prop.

Once the game is over, the king and the pawn
go back into the same box.

—Italian proverb

CHAPTER 22

Already

YOU WILL NOT OBTAIN GRACE at some future time because it has already been given to you. To pray for Grace to come is to deny that it has already come. It is not Grace you need to obtain. It is the *awareness* of the Grace already present. To affirm that you live in a state of Grace, and that all that could be given *has* been given, is to claim your rightful inheritance.

Jesus likened the kingdom of heaven to a banquet. He told the parable of a man who had prepared a feast and told his servant to invite the guests and tell them,

> Come, for all things are now ready.[1]

Jesus's parables were metaphysical teachings cloaked in common parlance the people of his time could understand. When he indicated that all things are now ready, he was speaking to all people for all time. He was erasing the time lag we perceive between what we have and what we want. He was saying that what you believe you need is *already* yours. He also stated explicitly:

The kingdom of heaven is at hand.[2]
and
The kingdom of heaven is within you.[3]

Jesus's awareness of the *alreadyness* of heaven was the power that enabled him to heal the sick, raise the dead, and perform miracles. In his mind and vision, the sick were *already* healed, the dead were *already* living, and the miracles were *already* done. In the kingdom of heaven—which is not a place, but a state of consciousness—there is no lack, sickness, or death. There is only wholeness, wellness, and life. Jesus's consciousness was so firmly established in the *already* kingdom of heaven that he lifted those he touched into it with him.

Jesus was not the only purveyor of the vision of heaven. All true prophets and seers of all religions and spiritual paths have invited the world to the banquet. Each of them taught according to their own context, culture, and metaphors. When everyone sits down together at the banquet, the costumes, labels, and religions they represent have been left at the door. All authentic roads lead to the light. Everyone comes home for the holidays.

No Prerequisites for Love

"Time is what keeps everything from happening at once," said novelist Ray Cummings. We might add, "Space is what keeps everything from happening here." Without the separating veils of time and space, life in all its fullness is happening here and now. Do not use time or space to distance yourself from what already is. You made up a story that what you need is elsewhere. You can just as easily—actually far *more* easily—make up a story that what you need is here now.

Heidi Baker is an impassioned minister who has taken it upon herself to help downtrodden people in Africa. In the documentary *The Finger of God*, we see Heidi on a mission in Lebanon, where she is joined by a Lebanese Christian evangelist. The two stand at the door of a sick woman who has requested prayer. The evangelist asks the woman, "Have you accepted Jesus Christ as your personal savior?"

The woman has not done so and she says she is not ready to do so. The evangelist tells her, "We cannot pray for you until you have accepted Jesus."

Heidi shakes her head and tells the man, "Of course we can pray for this woman. She needs help and she needs love. We can talk to her about Jesus afterward."

God's love is universal and unconditional, beyond any particular religion or belief system. The Lebanese evangelist would dole out healing only if the recipient did it *his* way. Heidi Baker would dole out healing because that's what love would do.

We all have our ideas about what we or others need to do first to deserve love, healing, or the good things in life. *None of these prerequisites are true*. There is no precondition you must fulfill to become worthy of what your heart desires and your soul deserves. You already merit healing, happiness, a rewarding relationship, financial prosperity, career success, and total well-being. The idea that you must earn love is the most debilitating distortion of truth that humanity has ever conjured. Human love is conditional. God's love is given fully and freely to all. When we love without condition or prerequisite, we become living expressions of God on earth and we bring earth closer to heaven. You have no other purpose than this.

Take a moment now to consider all the things you believe you or others need to do to earn love or receive Grace. The prayers you need to pray, the church services you need to attend, the donations you need to give, the people you need to help, the angry words you must never utter, the conditions you must rectify, the lust you must remove from your heart. What else do you believe you must do to be worthy of happiness? Here are some examples:

□ Be a good person
□ Follow all of your religion's commandments
□ Go to church, synagogue, or mosque
□ Resist chocolate and desserts
□ Get your parents to approve of you
□ Get your kids to follow your plan for them
□ Pay off your karma
□ Have someone forgive you
□ Master the Law of Attraction
□ Wait for astrological conditions to favor you
□ Lose ten pounds
□ Find your soulmate
□ Get rid of your soulmate
□ Get your next degree
□ Pay off your debts
□ Get cosmetic surgery
□ Get a prestigious job
□ Gratify your sexual attractions
□ Overcome your sexual impulses
□ Open all of your chakras
□ Find your guru
□ Live in Sedona
□ Retire
□ Get your book published

- ☐ Present a seminar for thousands
- ☐ Overthrow the evil government
- ☐ Have the messiah come
- ☐ Live to see extraterrestrials land
- ☐ Minimalize your life to bare necessities
- ☐ End pollution
- ☐ End starvation
- ☐ Create world peace
- ☐ Die and go to heaven

Fill in the blanks with your own list:

____

____

____

____

____

____

____

____

Regardless of what you have been told, you are enfolded in love *before* you achieve any of the above goals, or if you *never* do. Graceworthiness is a radical notion if you've been trained in a grace-earning mindset. If you devoted even a small portion of the energy you have invested in *earning* love, to *accepting* love, you would find yourself at heaven's door.

When you understand that wholeness resides within you, you become far more helpful to the world than when you believed you must keep rolling a rock up a hill. You might still pray, attend church, donate to worthy causes, volunteer to help people in need, work out, and perform many of the acts you felt obligated to do to buy your way into heaven. From the platform of sufficiency, however, your actions are *joy-motivated* rather than *fear-motivated*, which makes all the difference. When you proceed *from* Grace rather than *toward* it, you serve with exuberant creativity rather than guilt or a neurotic need to prove yourself or please others. *Why* you do things is more important than *what* you do. Doing things to avoid hell *is* hell. Doing things to express love *is* heaven. Love *finders* are far more powerful world change agents than love *seekers*. When you realize you abide in Grace, the world ceases to be a penal colony, a cosmic mistake, or a demanding school you need to earn or learn your way out of. It becomes a magnificent blank canvas upon which you paint a portrait of life as it was meant to be.

The Accelerator

I sometimes use a technique I find both mystical and practical. It is a tool to generate time collapse. If I am, let's say, hiking on a long nature trail and I find myself tiring on the way back, I throw my consciousness ahead to the moment I arrive back at my car. I imagine I am already there, relaxing and enjoying a drink and snack after the hike. In my mind it is already so. When I do this, the time it takes me to return to the car seems to diminish. Establishment in vision accelerates equivalent experience.

This exercise is a way of tricking the mind into a sense of completion. Fatigue is the offspring of resistance.

When I project my mind to a resistance-free condition, time dissipates, along with fatigue. Our experience of time depends on the thoughts we are thinking. When we focus with resistance on conditions we do not prefer, time solidifies and casts its net farther. When we step into thoughts and feelings of well-being, time loosens and lightens. Time is more like rubber than concrete.

The ultimate application of this exercise is to arrive at the place where all that we seek is already accomplished; all that we want is already given; all that we are striving for is already achieved; all that we yearn for, we already own; all that we hope to become, we already are. Such resolution makes no sense to the ego, which is based on seeking, needing, and traversing the *seeming* gap between where you are and where you want to be. The ego actively argues for emptiness and would not know what to do if it were not trying to make something different happen. So it creates an endless list of tasks we must achieve before we can relax. You can short-circuit the ego's brutal task-mastering by claiming wholeness now. "Already" is the mantra that opens the door to enlightenment. "Already" *is* enlightenment.

At this moment a sumptuous feast is offered you. But you must be willing to sit down and partake. *A Course in Miracles* reminds us, "There is no gift the Father asks of you but that you see in all creation but the shining glory of His gift to you."[4] The world was created not to imprison you, but to impassion you. The love and well-being you are waiting for tomorrow is here today. "Already" means that all is ready. Even while you traverse the globe in quest of things both menial and noble, you carry the sacred treasure inside your heart. The holy grail is already in your hand. Now you need but simply drink from it.

CHAPTER 23

Grace will Lead us Home

Through many dangers, toils, and snares
We have already come.
'Twas Grace that brought us safe thus far
And Grace will lead us home.
—From the song *Amazing Grace,* by John Newton

IF YOU CONSIDER all the things you have feared, worried about, and resisted over the course of your life, you will recognize that most of them did not happen. Of the few that did occur, the experience was not as bad as you expected. And of the events that proved harder, you came out on the other side. You grew from the experience and gained strength and character you would not have developed had your situation been easier. As you look back from a mature perspective, what seemed like a huge challenge at the time was but another step along the path—in many cases a very helpful one. In spite of your fears, upsets, and dramas, Grace has prevailed.

The Hand of Love that has guided you thus far will not abandon you now. Anxiety clouds your vision to make it appear that the current dilemma is different than the others and intrinsically more fearful, but *it is not.* Illusion finds exceptions to the presence of love, while truth reminds you that what is true is always true.

Reset

A nurse told me about a healing modality in which when a child is born, the parents freeze the placenta. If at a later age the child or adult becomes ill, cells are taken from the placenta and infused into the body. These cells contain the blueprint for the person's original pure state of health. They generate a reset mechanism that contributes to supersede any disease that has occurred since that time. The placenta cells represent restoring the individual to his or her original innocence.

If your computer crashes, you can press a *system restore* button that returns the computer's programs to a point that preceded the corruption. Deep within your computer's memory lies the record of all that was good and healthy before the problem occurred. By activating that memory, the defect is offset and well-being is renewed.

Likewise, deep within your soul you contain the memory of your original perfect self. That self has not been tainted by the world. It is the one part of you that is inviolate. It is the true you.

The 23rd psalm is a visionary journey into the heart of Grace. If you contemplate the psalm and absorb its far-reaching meaning, you will find safety, solace, and release. In the psalm we are told, *"He restores my soul."*

When you connect with Higher Power, you get your soul back. You can never really lose your soul; it is ever inviolate, eternal, and perfect. But you can lose touch with your soul. You can distance yourself from your awareness of the spiritual riches that you own and are. You can miss the *experience* of the wholeness it offers. When "He restores my soul," you are made new again. All the nightmares that seemed real disappear in the morning sunlight. You are still here, and all is well.

Your divine inheritance has been held in trust for you even while you have slept or denied it. At every moment it is yours for the asking. Your spiritual identity has not been sullied, damaged, or touched in any way by the pains and sorrows of life on earth. To the contrary, if your earthly journey has bought you more in touch with your soul, it has strengthened its reality.

You are not here by accident, and your sojourn has not been in vain. You cannot lose who and what you are. You have tried all manner of foolish attempts to import peace from sources outside yourself, and they have all failed. *Thank God*. There is but one place to find peace, and that is inside you. Grace has not allowed you to use an external object as a crutch. Kindness has redirected you to where your true strength lives. The world has never been your true home. Your kingdom is not geographical. It is spiritual.

What is yours by right of your spirit is yours forever. In the film *Bedazzled* (2000 version), a distressed young man named Eliot sells his soul to the devil in exchange for the granting of seven wishes. But after those wishes are granted, Eliot is no closer to peace, and the devil demands her due. While in jail awaiting the final dark judgment, Eliot meets a cellmate who is an angel in disguise. The fellow tells him, "Can't sell your soul anyway…because it doesn't really belong to you in the first place…It belongs to God."

Your soul, too, belongs to God, and God will take good care of it. The real you will not die and you will not go to hell. When love replaces fear, only heaven remains. Your only purpose on earth is to replace fear with love. When you do, Grace will lead you home.

Never underestimate the power of Grace to find you where you are and take your hand. No situation is so dark, dismal, or disgusting that Grace cannot enter and move you to higher ground. When you stepped outside the gate of the Kingdom, a homing device was implanted in your heart. That device has functioned perfectly, constantly feeding you information about where to turn, when, and how. The fact that you have often chosen not to listen to its message has not daunted it from broadcasting impeccable guidance. You know all you need to know when you need to know it.

Like the slave trader who awakened to the dignity of all people and wrote the famous song, Grace has brought you safe thus far, and Grace will lead you home. Do not lose heart and do not lose hope. Ultimately goodness prevails; that goodness is seeded within you and, despite appearances, it surrounds you. There is no place you could wander in the entire universe where Grace is not. You are loved and your homecoming is assured. Your destiny is to arrive at the place you began, and abide forever in the peace of God.

> You have not lost your innocence. . .This is the voice you hear, and this the call which cannot be denied. . .And now the way is open, and the journey has an end in sight at last. Be still an instant and go home with Him, and be at peace.
>
> — *A Course in Miracles*[1]

References

References to *A Course in Miracles* refer to the edition known as "The Only Complete Edition," Third edition published in 2007 by the Foundation for Inner Peace, P.O. Box 598, Mill Valley, CA 94942-0598, www.acim.org and info@acim.org.

As a shorthand reference to the numbering system in this edition, quotes labeled "T" refer to the Text, quotes labeled "W" refer to the Workbook for Students, and quotes labeled "M" refer to the Manual for Teachers. Numbers following the source indicate the chapter or lesson, section, paragraph, and line referred to.

From a Maze to Amazing

1. *A Course in Miracles*, T-1.I.6:1-2

Let Life Love You

1. Isaiah 11:6
2. *A Course in Miracles,* T-8.VIII.8:7
3. Shakespeare, William. *Julius Caesar,* Act 4, Scene 3

The Miracle of the Floating Fig

1. *A Course in Miracles,* T-2.V.A.18:5
2. www.bashar.org
3. *A Course in Miracles,* W, Lesson 76
4. Corinthians 13:11

The Face of God

1. Whitman, Walt. *Leaves of Grass: Songs of Myself.* Dover Publications (2007), 48

The End of Sin

1. *A Course in Miracles,* T-5.VI.10:2
2. John 8:7-11
3. *A Course in Miracles,* T-5.IV.8:2

The End of Punishment

1. *A Course in Miracles,* W-101.5:2
2. Shakespeare, William. *Romeo and Juliet,* Act 3, Scene 2
3. *A Course in Miracles,* W.fl.in.5:2

Grace Beyond Belief

1. Timothy 1:7
2. *A Course in Miracles,* T-14.XI.7:1
3. *A Course in Miracles,* W, Lesson 50

Who Walks with You

1. *A Course in Miracles,* T-18.III.3:2
2. *A Course in Miracles,* W-156.8:1-2
3. www.ramdass.org
4. Dass, Ram. *Be Here Now*. Lama Foundation (1978)
5. *A Course in Miracles,*W-337.1:5

The Ease Factor

1. LaPorte, Danielle. *Fire Starter Sessions*. Harmony (2014)
2. Matthew 6:25-29

Settle for More

1. *State of the American Workplace,* http://www.gallup.com/strategicconsulting/163007/state-american-workplace.aspx

Proof of Life after Debt

1. Cohen, Alan. *Enough Already*. Hay House (2012)
2. Shakespeare, William. *Hamlet*. Act 1, Scene 3
3. *A Course in Miracles,* W, Lessons 94, 110, 162
4. *A Course in Miracles,* W-78:1
5. *A Course in Miracles,* M-23.4:6
6. *Psalm 23*

When a Minus becomes a Plus

1. *A Course in Miracles, Manual for Teachers,* Section 4
2. Dabrowski, Dr. Kazimierz. *Personality Shaping through Positive Disintegration*. Red Pill Press (2015)

Good News for Control Freaks

1. Matthew 22:14
2. Ecclesiastes 3:1
3. *A Course in Miracles,* M-4.I.2:2

The Hard Questions

1. *USA Today,* http://usatoday30.usatoday.com/money/companies/management/2006-04-14-ceos-waiter-rule_x.htm

Pray with Your Feet Moving

1. *A Course in Miracles,* W, Lesson 24

Then a Miracle Happens

1. *A Course in Miracles,* W, Lesson 76

The Quality of Mercy

1. Shakespeare, William. *The Merchant of Venice*. Act IV, Scene 1
2. *A Course in Miracles,* T-1.I.45:1-2

Happy Outcomes Assured

1. *A Course in Miracles,* W, Lesson 292
2. Brother Lawrence. *The Practice of the Presence of God*. Whitaker House (1982)
3. Brother Lawrence. *The Practice of the Presence of God*. Whitaker House (1982)
4. Corinthians 13:12
5. Romans 12:2
6. *A Course in Miracles,* W.77:1

Already

1. Luke, 14:16-17
2. Matthew, 10:7
3. Luke, 17:21
4. *A Course in Miracles,* T-29.V.5

Grace will Lead us Home

1. *A Course in Miracles,* Excerpted from Lesson 182

Acknowledgements

I stand in humble gratitude to the God of Love Who sustains me and you and the entire universe. This book that celebrates Grace comes itself from Grace. I am thankful to all people and living things that have loved and supported me through this lifetime and others, especially those who have taught me the power of Grace by demonstrating kindness and forgiveness. I am extremely blessed, and I recognize the gifts I have received in so many ways.

More specifically, I thank my partner and beloved Dee who continually supports me to be all that I am, do all I am here to do, express my creativity, be happy, and walk the dogs.

I honor my esteemed mentor and friend Ram Dass for the inspiration he has given me for so much of my life, his untiring example of choosing love, and his kind endorsement for this book.

It has been a pleasure to co-create with Emma Sheppard, who has served so kindly and efficiently to format this book for publication.

I celebrate the talent of Maile Bongolon, who has created a magnificent cover befitting the energy and content of this book.

I thank you, reader, for opening to receive the gifts to which this book guides you, and extending Grace to yourself and those you touch. May the force of Grace continue to expand until we all realize how blessed we are.

About the Author

Alan Cohen, M.A., is the author of many popular inspirational books, including the best-selling *The Dragon Doesn't Live Here Anymore* and the award-winning *A Deep Breath of Life*. He is a contributing writer for the #1 New York Times best-selling series *Chicken Soup for the Soul*, and his monthly column, "*From the Heart*," is published in magazines internationally. His work has been featured on *CNN* and *Oprah.com* and in *USA Today*, *The Washington Post*, and the book *The Top 101 Experts Who Help Us Improve Our Lives*. His books have been translated into 24 languages.

Alan hosts the popular show *Get Real* weekly on Hay House Radio (hayhouseradio.com), and he has been a featured presenter in the award-winning documentary *Finding Joe*, as well as the documentaries *iGod* and *Living in Light*. Alan is the founder and director of the Foundation for Holistic Life Coaching, and he keynotes and presents seminars in the field of life mastery and vision psychology. He resides with his family in Hawaii.

For information on Alan Cohen's books, seminars, life coach training, DVDs, CDs, videos, and online courses, visit:

www.AlanCohen.com

Learn More with Alan Cohen

If you have enjoyed and benefited from *The Grace Factor,* you may want to deepen your understanding and inspiration by participating in Alan Cohen's in-person seminars, online courses, life coach training, or online subscription programs.

Quote for the Day—An inspirational quotation e-mailed to you each day (free)

Monthly e-Newsletter—Uplifting articles and announcements of events (free)

Wisdom for Today—A stimulating life lesson e-mailed to you daily

Online Courses—Lessons and teleseminars on relevant topics including relationships, prosperity, healing, prayer, metaphysics, *A Course in Miracles,* and time management

Mastery Training—A transformational retreat in Hawaii to align your life with your passion, power, and purpose

Life Coach Training—Become a certified professional life coach or enhance your career and personal life with coaching skills

For information about all of these programs and new products and events, visit:

www.AlanCohen.com.

82104818R00117

Made in the USA
San Bernardino, CA
13 July 2018